A MIRACLE A DAY
KEEPS THE DEVIL AWAY

BY PAT BOONE

The Real Christmas
A Miracle a Day Keeps the Devil Away

PAT BOONE

A MIRACLE A DAY
KEEPS THE DEVIL AWAY

FLEMING H. REVELL COMPANY
Old Tappan, New Jersey

Library of Congress Cataloging in Publication Data

Boone, Charles Eugene.
    A miracle a day keeps the Devil away.

    1. Miracles.   2. Boone, Charles Eugene.   I.   Title.
BT97.2.B63   248'.2   74-20772
ISBN 0-8007-0693-5

Then said the Lord unto Moses, Behold, I will rain bread from heaven for you; and *the people shall go out and gather a certain amount every day,* that I may test them, whether they will walk in my law, or not.

See Exodus 16:4

To my loving Father, the Eternal Source of daily miracles, this testimony is gratefully offered. Lord, please take these humble loaves and feed many.

CONTENTS

INTRODUCTION

The Japanese train hurtled through the tunnel at 150 miles per hour. I sat alone—in the middle of a Christmas concert tour—thinking about this book.

A book about miracles.

How could I explain the miracles in my life? If I told them in careful detail, documenting and explaining, leaving out nothing, would anybody understand? Does anybody still *believe* in miracles? What is a miracle—*anyway?*

A sudden flood of light shocked me out of my questioning, as the supertrain barreled into daylight and the Japanese countryside again. There was an accompanying roar, almost like a sonic boom, and from my window seat I saw that it had startled a group of small boys, playing in a circle some 100 yards or so from the track.

On an impulse, one of them waved.

Triggered by some similar impulse, I waved back.

Instantly, I felt foolish. But in that instant, the little boy had *seen* my wave! And as I flashed out of his life forever, he jumped up and down and waved at me—his fleeting, unknown friend—with boyish excitement.

I sat for a while, smiling in a warm silence, and then I thanked the Lord. He had just shown me something about miracles.

In my mind, I went back to that little circle of boys, playing in the field near the railroad track.

I saw my little friend whirl excitedly back into the circle, still jumping up and down, "He waved! He waved!"

I heard his pals laugh at him, "Oh, come on! Nobody waved at you—that big train? They don't even *see* us. Come on, let's play."

"No, he did—I *saw* him! I waved, and he waved back! Didn't you see it?"

The other little boys just laughed, and kidded their friend, while he began to feel a little embarrassed and grew quiet. Still—he looked down the track at the fast disappearing train and thought to himself, "He *did* wave at me. I know he did. I *saw* him."

He knew and I knew, and that was enough.

In a second of time, my world had touched his. It was a contact, a secret personal touch, just between him and me. I'll never forget it— it really happened—and I hope he'll remember it, too.

I hope that, in a little while, when God makes a secret personal contact with my little friend, he'll recognize and accept it. I hope he'll remember a faceless stranger, waving at him—at *him*—from a passing train, and know that even if all his friends reject his experience, he has touched God.

And God has touched him.

What's this got to do with miracles?

Well, this vivid momentary experience helps me to arrive at a simple definition of a miracle. Ready?

MIRACLE: *The Touch of God in your life.*

Oh, I know there are more complex, theological, philosophical, and all-encompassing definitions, including Noah Webster's: An extraordinary event taken to manifest the supernatural power of God fulfilling His purposes (such as the healings described in the Gospels).

But I'm going to stick to my simple definition, especially as I share with you thirty-one specific miracles that have happened to me, my family, and my friends. Some of the things I describe are startling, undeniable miracles—by *any* definition—and others may seem at first small and coincidental, perhaps, and unworthy of being thought of as miracles. But bear with me.

Because if God does it—*it's a miracle.*

Isn't it?

I mean, if He puts His divine finger into the course of human affairs *at any point,* and changes what would have happened into something different—that's a miracle!

Think about it with me. We live in a rational, material, scientific, practical, human world. We call it natural. Because man has achieved so much, just in this century, actually reaching into man to see how his brain works—and into outer space, to see how the universe works—our focus has been on humanity, on science, on technology, and man's natural abilities to do almost anything he can think of.

And it's become increasingly hard to focus on God. After all, God's not natural. He's *supernatural*. If—*if*—there is God—then He created all this, He set it in motion somehow, and He can *change* things, if He wants to.

He can operate within natural laws, or He can cut across and ignore them, if He chooses. But because He has that choice, and just because He *is*—*whatever* He does is supernatural, because He's doing it, and not man.

Is that right, or not?

It seems to me that anything God does that man couldn't—or didn't—do on His own, is supernatural. It's *more* than natural; it's something beyond man, it did not originate with man—and therefore, it's supernatural.

It's a miracle.

That's what prayer is all about.

If, by this simple definition, miracles don't happen today, you can forget prayer. It's a waste of time.

Here's a man praying for rain. If it doesn't rain soon, his crops will die, and he'll be ruined. So he prays. He earnestly asks God to cause it to rain, somehow, and he waits.

Right then, in Canada and over the Gulf of Mexico, high and low pressure areas are shifting in the atmosphere; massive cloud formations are being herded toward each other by unseen high winds—and soon, standing in his parched fields, the farmer lifts his face toward heaven and the first drops of rain roll down his cheeks with his grateful tears.

Natural—or supernatural?

If natural, then it was going to rain anyway, and the farmer should've saved his breath. His prayer was useless—a foolish exercise out of place in our modern, scientific age.

But—if at any point, whether in Canada or Mexico, or China or over the Arctic regions, or anywhere else, a listening God put His finger into the weather systems of the world and changed their pattern even slightly, to answer that man's earnest prayer—*we've got a miracle on our hands!*

I don't see any alternative. One of our basic scientific principles is the law of cause and effect; there is no action without an equal and opposite reaction; each thing that happens was caused by something else—and in turn, sets something else in motion. This principle dictates that the orderly universe has evolved from exploding matter over several billion years; that complex man has evolved steadily from simple one-celled animals; that civilization has evolved naturally from cave compounds to skyscrapers and supermarkets—all quite naturally. It's relentless, it's orderly, it's scientific—and very impersonal.

There's no room for prayer in that picture. It doesn't fit.

Prayer, if it worked at all, in any way, would call upon God to suspend this natural principle of cause and effect—and *change* things! It would ask Him to butt in, to rearrange, to block the inevitable, to reroute human events and confound scientific patterns, and this would be supernatural!

Wouldn't it?

So, if prayer makes any sense at all, if it truly contacts a living God who responds and answers, it is supernatural—and *miracles* become inevitable.

Jesus sparked miracles everywhere He went—changing the human condition every day, constantly rearranging things, speaking the impossible into existence. For Him, this was normal.

And He said, "Signs and wonders [miracles] shall follow *those who believe.*" (*See* Mark 16:17.)

Believe—believe what? The Good News, the Gospel (*see* vs. 15, 16), the fact that Jesus is God's Son, the Word become flesh, our open door to the Father, the sacrifice and forgiveness for our sin—and the Elder Brother to all who receive Him. The Apostle John says, "But as many as received him, to them gave he power to become the sons of God" . . . (John 1:12).

Believe Him when He says, "I'll be with you" (*see* Matthew 28:20); believe Him when He says, "My Father and I will manifest ourselves to you" (*see* John 14:21–23); believe Him when He says, "These things shall you do, and *greater than these shall you do,* because I go to be with my Father" (*see* John 14:12).

Believe other incredible promises like:

Matthew 3:11	Mark 10:28–30	Luke 4:17–19	John 7:37, 38
Matthew 5:1–12	Mark 11:24, 25	Luke 7:21, 22	John 10:9, 10
Matthew 6:3, 4, 31–33	Luke 1:37	Luke 10:17–20	John 16:23, 24

But the miracles are eternally linked to *belief*—don't forget that!

Recently, a college president said to my wife, Shirley, and me, "If I could have just one experience like you've had—*one* miracle—then I'd have to believe the way you do."

Then he paused and said, "Of course, I guess you'll say that if I believed, I *would* experience miracles—right?"

And I laughed and said, "That's right!" Jesus said, "These signs shall *follow* those who *believe!*" (*See* Mark 16:17.)

You know, so many people today worship (or run from) a God who is not described in the Bible! From Genesis to Revelation, *the only God you can read about is a miracle-working God,* a loving Creator who wants to be involved in the intimate details of His children's lives—who continually bails them out of their troubles; communicates with them personally and intimately; *changes* things in answer to their prayers—and rewards obedience.

If you spend much time at all getting to know the God of the Bible, you soon see a real Father, brooding over His kids, sometimes angry and hurt by their willful disobedience and fearful in His judgment—but also tender and forgiving and compassionate toward any individual who genuinely reaches up to Him in love and says, "I'm sorry, Father, I've made a mess of things, and it's because I tried to do it my way, not Yours. Please forgive me and help me—I need You."

Friend, I serve a mighty God who is also a compassionate Father. He's the One that Jesus pictures for us in the story of the prodigal son: the father running to meet his wayward child, kissing him, and embracing him, and preparing wonderful things to demonstrate his love.

I know and worship David's Shepherd, who fills my cup till it runs over, who anoints my head with oil, who guides and protects me and prepares a table before me *daily*—in the presence of my enemies.

My enemies.

Are you aware that you have enemies?

Do you have a sense that as you read this now you are being watched, that unseen opponents are muttering and fearful about the spiritual influence these words may have on you?

No? Does that sound too far-fetched, too medieval, too twilight-zonish? Is that idea even harder to swallow than our talk about miracles?

Well, I understand. And until I began to experience the miracles I would have scoffed at *both* ideas—the twin concepts of the miraculous and the satanic.

But they *are* unavoidably linked. And now you have the reason for the title *A Miracle a Day Keeps the Devil Away.*

There is a reason—a *need*—for miracles today. And it goes beyond God's desire to express His love for us and to strengthen our relationship with Him. Right now—as you read these words—you are already in the middle of a titanic, elemental life-and-death struggle between the forces of Good and Evil!

The battle has been raging for many centuries, and even though you didn't plan to get involved, you wandered innocently out onto the field and suddenly find it's happening all around you! Bombshells of tragedy are bursting everywhere, the sky is black with uncertainty and fore-boding, familiar landmarks have been blasted and changed, cries for help are heard from injured and frightened and dying people—and as the casualties mount, so few seem able to help.

Hardly anybody really knows what's going on. Who knows where these invisible bullets are coming from? Who's shooting at us? And why? Why are we the *targets* in this devilish situation anyway? Can't men just learn to love each other and work out their problems peacefully? Can't we call a truce somehow and solve man's dilemmas through arbitration, through sharing and caring, through some rational approach? If only the earthquakes, the hurricanes, the famines, the disease and "natural" disasters would let up for a while . . . .

Maybe, like so many of us, you've tried to dodge the battle, reason or ignore it away. You've ducked into a foxhole or maybe a comfortable bunker almost out of sight and sound of the sorrow and death raging uncontrolled on life's horizon. A good job, a decent community, occasional (or even regular) church attendance, a better-than-average moral outlook—all these lull you into a sense of security and the comforting thought that you and your loved ones are okay. You'll "get by"—you're "making it."

Then—a heart attack! A job is gone just overnight! The house burns! A child is run over! Cancer—in your family! The store is robbed, a plane goes down, a girl is pregnant! A wife is raped, an old man bludgeoned.

Why, God, why? Why *me,* God? Why *my* child, God?

And the battle has come to you.

You have become a target, even in that "secure" foxhole, and you're wounded. You're terribly frightened; you don't understand this war at all; and you're not even sure whose side you're on. Perhaps, like many, you blame God. Who else is there, anyway? *Who can you blame if not God?*

Good question.

And if you're seriously asking, and really want to know something of the fundamental basics of this worldwide all-encompassing showdown we're in—please get your Bible right now, before we go any further—and read these few passages: Genesis 3; Exodus 3:1–12 and 7:8–22; Matthew 4:1–11 and 24; 8:16, 17 and 28–34; 10:1; 16:13–26; Ephesians 6:10–18; and 1 Peter 5:6–11.

I know I've just given you a pretty stiff spiritual prescription. Few people are used to reading that much Scripture in one sitting—and you may not have taken the time and trouble to look up and read those passages yourself, yet. But I've pointed them out to you, and I pray you will read them carefully. They'll answer a lot of your questions—probably create new ones.

Good. The Bible can answer those too!

You see, I've just referred you to the *Manufacturer's Handbook*— the *Owner's Manual*—God's Word. That's where the answers are, and that's where you'll find out what this life-battle is all about—and how you can be on the winning side! If you read what I've outlined above, you'll see a continuing conflict between God and Satan that erupted before Eden and boils nonstop right into today, with human beings the prize, the target—and the battlefield!

You'll begin to understand why I want to share with you the miracles that happen daily in my life. The things I'm about to tell you have actually *happened* to me, my family, and friends. I know they're true, and they've radically affected my personal relationship with my loving God.

They've also greatly strengthened me for my daily battle with the Devil! And I hope they'll help you, too.

Every morning I feel like David going out to meet Goliath. I face a real giant, a real army of enemies—and yet, I'm no more afraid than David was!

Why?

Because I've got the same winning combination *he* had. David knew he was on God's side, he was willing to stand up and fight—and *he expected a miracle.*

I've gladly placed myself on God's side, I'm willing to do what I can —and I expect a miracle *every day!*

This book relates thirty-one of those miracles. You might read just one a day for a month, and think about it; or you may race on through in a hurry.

Either way, my prayer is that you'll begin to see that God is touching your life already, that He's waving at you from the train, reaching out in love through this speeding universe to *change* things where you are.

You and I are involved already in the same struggle, and it's do or die. We face the same enemy, and grapple with many of the same fears and dangers and devices. But we have the same God and Saviour, too! And He loves us with the same overflowing love—what He's done for me and my family, He wants to do for you!

And He will, I know.

Very soon now, you'll be experiencing your own miracle a day.

PAT BOONE

Revelation 12:9–11

A MIRACLE A DAY
KEEPS THE DEVIL AWAY

1 MY FIRST MIRACLE

I'd like to tell you about the first miracle I remember.

It happened when I was five, and I'll just bet something similar happened to you during that very vulnerable period of *your* life.

I was out riding my tricycle on the sidewalk in front of our house in Nashville, Tennessee. As I remember, it was the middle of the afternoon and I still have the vague impression Mama was very involved in her housework and couldn't be bothered right then with watching how Number One Son was becoming the Evel Knievel of our block.

As kids do, I was imagining myself in thrilling competition, racing to put out fires, winning the Kentucky Derby (I didn't realize my tricycle would have been disqualified), and helping Superman in various ways. I was having a ball, but after a while I realized I had just about reached the zenith, the optimum, of performance—mine and the machine's. It just would not go any faster, no matter how hard I pumped, or how I ducked my head to cut down on wind resistance, or how I huffed and puffed, or *anything!*

Unless . . . wait a minute! There was that wonderful sloped driveway! It dropped down, right at the sidewalk, and made a neat paved hill all the way to the street running past our house. Perfect! Now I could *really* get some speed!

Without a further thought, or a look up or down the street, I pedaled to the driveway and turned down it, heading toward the bottom and anticipating the thrill in the pit of my stomach as I gathered momentum. But suddenly I was dangling in midair watching my precious tricycle rolling from under me, watching it roll faster and faster, watching it reach the bottom and race right out into the street in front of an oncoming bus!

I watched it crumpled and smashed under the big tires of the bus—and for one sickening, numbing moment felt that I was still on it!

But I wasn't. I was being gently placed on the sidewalk now by a big teenaged boy from up the street, Graham MacPherson. He just happened to be walking by at that precise moment, saw that I was about to make a tragic mistake, and *acted* instead of speaking. If he hadn't, I'd most likely have been killed right there.

I don't remember what happened for a while after that. I don't know what Mama's reaction was, what the bus driver said, whether I cried for my tricycle, or anything else. But I'll never forget Graham MacPherson —or his warm smile that assured me everything was okay.

Didn't something like that happen to you? Don't you remember a time when you barely escaped death or serious injury, when some crazy little quirk, or a passing stranger saved you from onrushing tragedy? When, "but for the grace of God . . . ."

The "grace of God." How easy it is for us to say that! It sounds so comfortably general and vague. It's almost like saying "as luck would have it" or "in the providence of heaven," or "fortune smiled on me." Why can't we just say, in great, glad gratitude, *"God saved me!"*?

Did you know that's what *Jesus' Name means,* in Hebrew? His very name, *Jehoshua,* which the Greeks shortened to *Jesus,* means literally "Jehovah is salvation"—or *God saves!*

And everywhere He went, Jesus lived up to His Name. He said, "If you've seen Me, you've seen the Father" (*see* John 14:9), and He proved that God was interested in the practical, personal, immediate needs of our lives—*every* day! He fed the hungry, healed the sick, answered the questions, supplied the finances, changed the water to wine. He wasn't afraid to be specific. In fact, in Mark 11:24 and John 14:13, He expressly urges us to ask *anything* in His Name, and if we're really believing Him —JEHOVAH IS SALVATION—our God will do it for us!

Not just "grace," or "luck," or "providence" or "fortune"—but *God, Himself,* for us!

Read how David described a "lucky" or "fortuitous" moment in his life, when King Saul, who was trying to find David to kill him, just "happened" to come into the very cave where David was hiding—and lay down to take a nap! You'll find it in 1 Samuel 24, and be sure you read verse 10. The great people in the Bible knew where their help was coming from, and they weren't afraid to be personal and specific about it.

No, Graham MacPherson didn't just "happen" along. God saved my life that afternoon in my fifth year, and He nudged Graham into the right spot at the right time. He may even have commissioned an angel to look after it.

Oh, yes, there *are* guardian angels. Paul says specifically in Hebrews 1:14:

> Are they [angels] not all ministering spirits, sent forth to minister for them who shall be heirs to salvation?

---

1 Samuel 24   Hebrews 1:14
John 14

2 GOD'S WAKE-UP SERVICE

God has a great sense of humor!

He made this very clear to me early in my miracle walk with Him, and I'd like to share the story with you.

I'd just come in from some out-of-town trip, and tiptoed into the bedroom right at 3:00 in the morning! As I shelled out of my clothes and slid wearily into bed, Shirley woke up long enough to ask me what time I wanted to get up (she knew she'd have the thankless job of trying to pry me out of the bed in the morning).

I remembered a very important 9 A.M. meeting I had to make, so after a few seconds' calculation of all the shortcuts I might manage, I answered, "Oh, 8:15, I guess."

Shirley sort of muttered, "You'll never make it, but okay," turned over, and was quickly asleep again. In a few seconds, I knew, I'd be dead to the world, too, and I mentally projected ahead to nine that morning and saw a bunch of very important people looking at their watches and beginning to be upset with Pat Boone. I realized that under my own steam I'd never make it on time! Not getting up at 8:15.

And yet I was absolutely exhausted; I *had* to have that five hours sleep, didn't I? What could I do?

I'd just been reading John 14:14 where Jesus says, "Ask *anything* in my name . . . ," and I wondered if He would include something as seemingly trivial as getting up in the morning and making an important meeting on time. I decided to find out.

As I said, this was early in my new relationship with the Lord, and I wasn't even certain that He was listening to me. So, in sort of a tentative whisper, I said, "Jesus—are You there?

"May I ask You something?

"You know how tired I am, Lord, and yet I do have that meeting at nine. Shirley's going to wake me up at 8:15, but You know me—I'm not one of those push-button, instant-action people in the morning, even after a *good* night's sleep!

"If You don't help me get up and get moving fast in the morning, I'll just never make it. Will You help me, Jesus?

"I'm trying to believe that You hear me, and that You care and will be involved in the real things of my life, so I'm going to thank You in advance—okay?

"I believe You'll help me—so thank You, Jesus."

And Z-Z-Z-Z-Z-Z-Z-Z—I was gone! Out like a light!

Seven o'clock came, and Shirley eased out of bed (after stifling the alarm clock with a lightning move—that's the way she is, faster than a speeding bullet)—and was dressed in minutes, flashed down the stairs and hustled breakfast like a short-order cook, got the four girls bundled into the car and off to school—and arrived back home just at 8:15!

For several weeks before this, she'd been listening to Kathryn Kuhlman's radio program at that time of the morning, and the stories of miracles she'd been hearing had greatly increased Shirley's hunger to get closer to Jesus. But *this* particular morning, Kathryn wasn't interviewing someone who'd experienced a miracle; she was reading a long passage from the Bible, and was about to make a point which Shirley didn't want to miss!

So she ran in the kitchen door and punched the stereo button (one of several we have around the house), knowing that the radio, turned already to Kathryn's station, KHOF, would come on right away—and that there was a speaker *right by our bed!* That way she'd wake me up and not miss the point Kathryn was about to make. (Smart gal, huh?)

Now, that particular morning, *at that particular time,* Kathryn Kuhlman was reading from chapter 5 of Ephesians, and just as the radio blared on (almost in my ear) at 8:15, she reached the fourteenth verse —and in her punctuated, very definite voice she commanded, "Awake, thou that sleepest . . ."

"AWAKE—THOU THAT SLEEPEST!"

I got up. No, I *jumped* up! I moved around like a man leaving a burning building—and I was at that meeting on time!

Later, of course, I laughed. And I toyed with the idea that it was just a hilarious coincidence.

I mean—to *ask* God for something is one thing; but to *get* such a specific, pointed, incredible *answer* is something else! I don't mind telling you it scared me a little, and to believe it was a coincidence would have been comforting.

But I'd been in Las Vegas, and had once stupidly gambled some money away. I'd learned, the hard way, a little about "odds." What were the odds against my making a specific request at 3 A.M., and having all those unusual, disconnected circumstances—including Kathryn's arriving at that one verse out of the whole Bible—and Shirley's waking me up with the stereo (which she'd never done before)—converge to wake me up that way *at the precise moment* I'd requested? By coincidence?

A trillion to one, maybe?

No, I ruled out coincidence. God had heard me. I knew, 'way down deep, that He was listening to Pat Boone.

And that He had a great sense of humor.

I can't really tell you how much those two things meant to me, as they began to soak in. At that point in my mixed-up life, I was going to need many miracles, and the memory of this tingling moment would kindle my faith and help me through some terrible knotholes. And at times when I'd be tempted to cry in despair and self-pity—like a little alarm clock, this episode would ring in my spirit and make me laugh. What a wonderful Lord I was coming to know!

"Awake, thou that sleepest."

And I was awaking, at last—to a God of miracles.

Matthew 6:6–8   Matthew 7:7–11

3   A ROOM IN HARLEM

The New York police begged us not to come.

But we were about to film David Wilkerson's story *The Cross and the Switchblade,* and we wanted to film it on the very streets and in the actual parts of New York where it had originally taken place. We wanted realism, and you really can't recreate the ghettos of Harlem and Fort Greene in Hollywood—or anywhere else.

But violence still raged, and drugs were king. Though organized street gangs were on the decline, murder wasn't. To get money for the next fix, desperate junkies, from early teens to old-timers, were attacking women, taxi drivers, priests, *anybody*—with no warning. And it was getting worse.

The cops laid it on the line. "We cannot protect you. We can't prevent your coming, but your lives are in danger, and we advise you to film somewhere else."

Still we came—in prayer—Dick Ross and Tom Harris and Don Murray and I, believing that the God who protected Dave Wilkerson the first time around while he was living his fantastic adventure in those streets would protect us, as we attempted to recreate it on film. We were scared, sure, but looking for miracles!

They happened.

Don Murray, who had earlier written and directed the prizewinning *Hoodlum Priest,* came in early to look for locations. With the help of some Teen Challenge graduates, ex-street hoods, and a plainclothesman, he walked through the roughest areas of the Bronx, Simpson Street, Fort Greene (Brooklyn), and deepest Harlem, picking out spots and parks and alleys that had the right look for the story.

The outdoor spots weren't too difficult to find and make arrangements for, but the indoor places were. Space is at a premium in a ghetto, and people are naturally suspicious of others and protective of what little they have. Nobody wanted some Hollywood creeps coming in and poking around in their private quarters—they had *enough* trouble!

Don understood, and was very sympathetic. He never pushed anybody; he just kept looking. Tom Harris, associate producer and an ex-fighter, joined Don at that point, and together they knocked on doors around 136th Street in Harlem, searching for a basement room big enough to become the headquarters for the Mau Maus, formerly the most vicious gang in New York City. Since Nicky Cruz, its leader, had become a Christian through Wilkerson's tenacious prayers for him, the gang had disbanded. But Don had to recreate the gang for the film, and a major part of the story centered in this important location. It had to have just the right look and feel.

After a number of near-misses, they found it. Some neighborhood kid told them about a big basement boiler room that was serving right then for a large local gang, or "club;" as its "clubhouse." Don and Tom met with the top guys in that club and persuaded them to let it be used in our film. With a little painting and rearranging, it would have just the atmosphere the script called for.

In a few days, we began our filming there. I don't mind telling you I was scared. Especially after getting in a cab the first day, giving him the address of the location and having him tell me, "You gotta be crazy, Mac! They killed a *priest* up there the other day! Whattaya wanta go there for?"

I told him I was making a movie, playing a priest, or minister.

"You're outa your mind! Look, I'll take ya. But pay me now, and when we get there, I'll let ya out quick—*fast*, y'understand? And don't ask me t'come back for ya."

The first couple of days, we shot outdoors. And though large crowds gathered, there was no real trouble. One afternoon, filming across from a welfare office, Don and I had to go march in a picket line for fifteen minutes so that the picketers would quiet down and let us get our filming done. We did it, and they kept their part of the bargain. And, with the exception of occasional appeals from strung-out local junkies for handouts, things went smoothly.

Eventually, we went indoors, and began the first of many scenes in the gang hangout. That first day, we shot the initial meeting between the frightened young preacher and Nicky Cruz, the psychotic "garbage-can killer." He'd been called that because Nicky used to put a garbage can over his head—with a slit cut in it so he could see—and wade into gang fights with a switchblade and a long pipe with a plumbing fitting on the end. He doesn't know today how many people he "wasted."

I was feeling pretty inadequate to portray Dave Wilkerson. The gang kids were New York actors, black and Puerto Rican, and many of them had actually been street fighters and still bear scars today from their own gang wars. I was feeling real Hollywood in that smoke-blackened dingy room—when in walked David Wilkerson himself!

He'd just been able to shake loose from his crusade work for a couple of days, and had flown in to see what we were "doing with his life." He understood my shakiness, and we prayed and talked together. Quickly, I began to feel more confident, and he stood back and watched us film a heavy scene.

Once we had it, and the crew was setting up for the next shot, Don Murray and I talked to David. "Who told you about this place?" Dave asked.

Don chuckled, and answered, "Nobody—almost. We practically had to dig it out with our bare hands. We began to think we weren't *ever* going to find a spot with the right look and size and feel. Honestly, we wondered if such a place still existed in Harlem . . . ." And he went on to tell about the long search.

Dave's face grew even more serious than usual, and he leaned in.

"You mean nobody told you that *this is the very room where I met my first gang?*"

I'll never forget what I felt in that moment. Neither will Don. Or Dave.

Nobody *had* told us, because nobody around us knew. Except one. Guess who?

The One who brought Dave Wilkerson to New York City in the first place!

Jesus led a skinny young preacher to that very room thirteen years before to prove to thousands of ghetto victims that a loving God cared about them. And Jesus had unerringly led a scared young actor back to that basement boiler room in Harlem—so that a film could take that same message to millions!

Yea, though I walk through the valley of the shadow of death, I will fear no evil: for thou art with me; thy rod and thy staff they comfort me. Thou preparest a table before me in the presence of mine enemies: thou anointest my head with oil; my cup runneth over. Surely goodness and mercy shall follow me all the days of my life: and I will dwell in the house of the Lord for ever.

Psalms 23:4–6

4 MIRACLE OF THE MOUSE

"Daddy, please—can you take me to the vet right away?"

My second daughter, Lindy, then fourteen, who reminds me so much of an Indian princess in her dark beauty, stood before me, giant tears filling her eyes. In her cupped hands she held a little brown mouse, curled up and still, apparently lifeless. It had been a Christmas present from her best friend, and was precious to her already.

I looked at the wee creature, saw just the faintest trace of breathing, and experienced that familiar sinking feeling a parent knows when a child asks so earnestly for something that's probably impossible. And yet —I looked up again into those big, brown, brimming-over eyes of Lindy's, anxious and hoping and imploring, and knew I had to try.

But what?

"I'll call the guy at the pet store and see what he says." Lindy followed me to the phone in the pantry, still holding the mouse in the cup of her hands.

The man at the store laughed when I told him the problem. "I'm sorry," he said, "but it *is* sort of funny. There's nothing anybody can do. Just throw it in the trash and come on down. We'll give you another one. A sick mouse is a dead mouse."

Throw it in the trash? He obviously couldn't see the look on Lindy's face. I thanked him and phoned the vet, Dr. Miller.

Again, I could sense the amusement on the other end of the line. "Oh, no, Mr. Boone, there's no point in bringing the mouse over here. I couldn't help you. You should probably just replace it."

I thanked him for his time and hung the phone up, feelings clashing inside me. Part of me wanted to stage a grand burial (we'd done that before with Debby's iguana) and then go pick out a new mouse, maybe two.

But another part of me was reaching desperately to God, asking Him for a miracle—*now!*

"Come on, Lindy, let's go upstairs." She knew I meant we were going to the bedroom to pray. Little Laury, our youngest, had joined us, having instant empathy for Lindy and the mouse, and wanting to help any way she could.

On the way up the stairs, I thought, *"What* am I *doing?* That little mouse is almost dead. Why should I risk Lindy's faith this way? Is God really concerned about such a trivial thing—and what will it do to my daughters if He doesn't do something?"

Still, it seemed the only chance we had, and in a moment we had closed the bedroom door and 'were kneeling around the bed, crying out to the Lord.

"Father, didn't Jesus teach us to bring our every concern to You? Didn't He say that You take notice of every bird and flower, and number the very hairs on our heads? And didn't He actually say that if we had enough faith we could speak to a mountain and see it moved into the sea?

"Well, Lord, we believe Your Word.

"And right now, we're not concerned with a mountain. It's this little mouse. Nobody can help it but You, Lord. The pet store man can't, and the vet can't, and we can't. Only You, Lord. And You made this little animal—You must love it more than we do. Please, heal this little thing, give it life."

Something I'd been reading just that morning in John's Gospel flashed before me. "Jesus, remember when You called Lazarus from the tomb? Just before You commanded the dead man into life, You *thanked God out loud* in front of everybody, because You knew He was hearing You! Well, Lord, we know You hear us, and so we want to thank You right now."

And we did. For a couple of minutes, it seemed so right to just thank the Lord and express our love to Him. Our hands went up in the air, as if bearing a literal gift to our Father, and tears of real joy ran down our cheeks. It was not till later that I learned Lindy had felt the mouse twitch *just as we began to thank the Lord,* and she had tearfully placed him on the bed without opening her eyes. Not knowing if it was living or dead, she gave herself to praise, thanking God for His goodness.

And somehow, together, we *knew!*

We opened our eyes and right before us on the corner of the bed, that little mouse was sitting up, weakly rubbing its face with its front feet!

It seemed awfully shaky, but while we watched, laughing and crying and praising God all at the same time, it appeared to gain strength every minute! Lindy ran and brought back some seeds and lettuce, but though it made a feeble attempt to crack a seed, the little mouse seemed still too weak and just nibbled a little lettuce and drank some water that Laury had brought.

In a couple of minutes, though, it rummaged around for a seed it had shoved under itself for future reference and cracked it and began to eat! That was all we needed to see—we knew it was just a matter of time—that the patient was on the road to recovery. And sure enough, in just a little while, the Miracle Mouse (that's what we named it) was running around like crazy, more full of life than ever!

But wait—that's not all.

Lindy began to cry again, even while we knelt by the bed, watching the mouse regain its strength. "What's the matter, honey?" I asked her.

"Daddy," she answered, when she could sort of get herself together. "I just realized that God has answered another prayer, probably more important than our prayer for the mouse.

"A few days ago, some of my friends and I got into a big discussion about God, and this boy, a couple of years older than the rest of us—and very smart—laughed at us and showed us in some pretty logical-sounding ways that there couldn't be a God. I really didn't believe him, but I didn't have answers that could change his mind, and I did sort of feel foolish.

"I stopped praying for a couple of days, and really have been feeling sort of confused and lousy and irritable—and separated from God and you all, too."

The tears started rolling again, but she continued, "Just yesterday I prayed, 'God, if You're there, and hear me, please show me that You're real. And dear God, show me in some way that's *not logical!*'

"Daddy, I know that's why this happened. God *does* hear me and He *does* answer our prayers, and we just can't *ever* understand that with our logic, can we?

"Thank you, Daddy."

Well . . . my hands went up again, and looking heavenward through my own flowing tears I cried, "Thank You, Father." (*See* Romans 8:15.)

Things were different around our house after that. We were much more bold about coming to God in faith, trusting Him with anything and everything. And eventually, reading again the story of Lazarus, I saw that the reason for his miracle and ours was the same—"that you might see the glory of God" (*see* John 11:40).

And He will still manifest that glory, whether He uses a man—or a mouse.

Matthew 6:24–34   John 11

5 THE MIRACLE OF NOW, INC.

Once in a while I get some criticism from well-meaning folks about the fee I have to charge when I sing or speak. Especially when the sponsoring organization is a Christian or charitable one.

"But we're giving you an opportunity to *minister*," they say, "and to *help* somebody. You shouldn't look at this as one of your career activities."

Well, I understand their point of view.

And they're right—they are giving me a chance to *minister*, and I love it. I love to share with others the wonderful goodness of God, to tell people what He's done for me, and to sing all kinds of songs about it.

But there's another side to that story, and some of my critics aren't aware of it. Without going into unnecessary details, I'll just say that there are considerable expenses involved in maintaining an entertainer's career, whether he's charging for his services or not. Airlines aren't giving free passes, hotels still charge, secretaries still get salaries when the boss is gone, agents and managers and accountants and lawyers still get fees—and lots of stuff like that.

And more and more, my career activities include speaking and singing for Jesus all over the country—and in other countries, too. Obviously, an orderly system had to be arrived at. So, a couple of years ago I formed an association with a fine Christian agent, Wayne Coombs, and asked him to develop a plan for including as many "Jesus events" in my travel schedule as possible.

The fee (though far less than my entertainment one) became an important part of the plan, not only to make it possible expense-wise, but to help us know which of the hundreds of invitations to accept. We've prayed from the beginning that God would use this reasonable fee to spotlight the exact place He wanted me to be—and according to His timetable.

All of this preamble is necessary to set the stage for the Miracle of NOW, Inc.

I believe this incredible happening illustrates the truth that "with God all things are possible" (Mark 10:27 and Matthew 19:26), and that when Jesus promised in Matthew 18:19, ". . . if two of you shall agree on earth as touching any thing that they shall ask, it shall be done for them of my Father which is in heaven"—He didn't set an age limit on it!

My family and I were in the middle of a singing tour last year, with a busload of musicians, other singers, managers, and assorted "road people." We were appearing in major cities, entertaining large crowds, mixing our "pop" songs with various kinds of Jesus music, and feeling good about the whole thing. It was early on a Sunday afternoon, and we were pulling into a small Tennessee town to do a very rare matinee performance which Wayne Coombs had arranged.

The sponsoring organization was NOW, Inc.

Wayne hadn't told us much about the group, but he said they had asked for a regular family show, and they specifically wanted us to do some Jesus music and share freely our Christian experience. They had happily accepted the fee requirement, and seemed to want to offer our program to the community. It certainly had a happy feel to it, and I just assumed NOW, Inc. was a group of concerned local businessmen.

The bus rolled up to the high-school football stadium about an hour before show time, and the guys with us jumped off to start setting up the sound equipment and checking the stage. There were just a handful of young people standing around in the bright sun, and I got off to take a look at the big empty stands, and find one of the sponsors to fill me in on just what was going to happen.

The kids standing around said, "Praise the Lord, Brother Pat."

"Right! Praise the Lord!" I responded. "Say, can you tell me if there's anyone here from NOW, Incorporated?"

"Sure—that's us. *We're* NOW, Incorporated."

A moment of stunned silence.

"You're . . . you kids . . . you're the whole thing? You're NOW?"

"Well, there's nine of us, actually, but a couple of the guys haven't gotten here yet. But they'll be here in a minute, and it's gonna be great here today. We've really been praying about this, and the Lord's gonna do His thing for our whole town. You and your family are an answer to prayer!"

Now it was *our* turn, our whole busload, to sort of stand around in the sun, wondering what in the world we were doing there—looking at empty stands, less than an hour from the announced time, discovering that *nine high-school and college kids* had incorporated, raised the deposit by odd jobs and small donations, negotiated the contract with Wayne Coombs, had posters printed and plastered all over town, and built a stage out on the football field!

"But . . . ," I hesitated a second. "Where are the people?"

There was such cheer and confidence in their answer. "Oh, don't worry. They'll be here. We've spent much time in prayer and fasting about this, and the Lord showed us that He's with us. We believe Mark 11:24! Don't worry."

I looked at those eager, trusting faces—and just started laughing. I mean, I really laughed. But it wasn't in derision, or skepticism, or as if I were in the middle of a big impossible bad joke.

I laughed because I *believed* them!

And loved them. And knew, somehow, that it was going to work. There *would* be people in those stands, and the Lord *was* gonna do His thing, and that God Himself was probably delighted at the audacious faith of these young Tennessee Jesus people who *dared* to believe His Word.

And sure enough, while we were all standing there laughing and praying and praising the Lord, the people started streaming in. They came in cars and busses and pickup trucks, and walking across the highway, and on motorbikes. Businessmen and farmers and housewives and school teachers, whole families and little kids, lots of church folks and plenty of curious people who hadn't been to a church in years. Nobody quite knew what to expect, but nobody wanted to miss it!

By the time we began the music, almost four thousand people had filled the stands and spilled out onto the playing field, sitting on the grass as happy as jaybirds!

What a time we had!

The musicians never played better; our black friends, the McCrarys, never sang better; Miss Tennessee appeared to sing and tell of her love for Jesus; and Shirley, the girls, and I felt like we were at a home-coming.

The people clapped and sang and raised their hands in the ONE WAY sign and heard us tell some of the marvelous things that had happened to us since God moved into our house. Each of my daughters told what the living Jesus meant to her, and while God painted the Tennessee sky with one of the most beautiful sunsets in human history, we concluded with a tearful musical prayer of commitment: "I Have Decided to Follow Jesus."

It was a very special day—and we all knew it. God was there.

Now, there are a couple of footnotes to that story.

One is that NOW (No Other Way, Incorporated) didn't meet their budget that day. Even with all those people. The kids, with their big hearts and lack of any promotional experience, had woefully underpriced the tickets, and then had let lots of people, especially children, in free! This meant that they had to pray some more, and take some more after-school jobs, and round up some more donations from the community to meet their obligations. Wayne and I did what we could to lighten the load for them, but it still took months to pay off all the expenses.

Still, they did it. And their town is still talking about that afternoon, and what NOW, Incorporated did. Hearts were touched, and lives changed. And that's what those nine Jesus kids were praying for—not just a show—but for changed lives! They were praying for revival, for a manifestation of the Lord in their town (John 14:23). And He answered their prayers.

The other footnote is from the Bible. Read John 6:1–14, and you'll see the parallel. You'll see Jesus receiving what one young boy offered Him—and feeding five thousand people! And right out on the grass, too! He's the same wonderful Lord today.
NOW!

The Kingdom of Heaven is like a treasure a man discovered in a field. In his excitement, he sold everything he owned to get enough money to buy the field—and get the treasure, too!

See Matthew 13:44

6   WHAT DO YOU SAY TO A JEWISH PORNOGRAPHER?

"Hey, Boone, I read your book!"
I cringed.
(Normally, I'm delighted to hear someone say they've read *A New Song*—delighted to know the Lord has provided another opportunity for me to share my story.)
But—a *Jewish pornographer?*
In the steam room at the Sands Hotel?
In Las Vegas?

I sensed a punch line coming, and braced myself for it. But none came. The squat, curly-haired man whose current business was selling pornographic material and actual grotesque sex machines was looking at me earnestly.

"You're serious about this whole thing, aren't you?" he asked.

I nodded, still apprehensive, "Sure I am. Where in the world did you get hold of my book?"

"From Frankie Avalon." (I had given several copies to entertainer friends, including Frankie, Dean Martin, Bob Goulet, and Johnnie Ray —but *not* to anybody I thought might find it "weird" or just joke material, like Ace here, the gregarious, profane, trafficker in sordid sex gimmicks! I guess he'd be the *last* guy in Las Vegas I'd have shared my story with—and now we stood dripping and steaming together, with several friends looking on in disbelief.)

"I'd like you to pray for me!" he said, softly.

I guess everybody's jaws dropped, including mine. Was this guy joking? Was he setting me up for something?

"I mean it. I always thought this religion stuff of yours was some kind of phony trip, just part of your 'image'—you know. But the book really got to me. It really did.

"Look, I know why my life is so messed up. I'm my own worst enemy. I've been married four times, bankrupt twice, and if I knew some other way to make a living, I wouldn't be selling this junk. I sure ain't proud of it.

"Look, I'm fat, flabby, and over forty, and now the doc tells me I've got to go in for a gall bladder operation—and I'm scared to death.

"I'd really like you to pray for me."

I could swear I felt goose bumps in that 170 degree wet heat!

"Look, Ace," I said, not daring to glance at the other guys, "I'll be happy to pray for you. I will. But you know, God wants to hear from *you* about your problems. That's really the whole idea. Will you pray, too?"

The look on his face seemed a mixture of sadness and hilarity, if you can imagine such a thing. The twin forces rushed together and erupted into a loud laugh, as he said, "Me? *Pray?* Oh, come *on*—God would strike me dead, tell me to get lost or go to hell, or something! You gotta be kidding!"

I sensed a real loneliness, a vacuum in this man, and suddenly saw the hard, gruff exterior for what it was—a disguise.

"Ace," I said, obeying an inner impulse before I quite realized how rash it was, "so many people have the wrong idea about prayer and about God Himself. He's not interested in just hearing religious words from so-called religious people. Jesus Himself said there was only one really *good* person—and that was God! So God wants to hear from each one of us, not because we're good, but because He just plain ol' *loves* us!

"Look, I didn't arrange for you to read my book. I would have tried to keep it *away* from you, figuring you wouldn't dig it at all. So God must have wanted you to read it, and made it possible. He knows your heart a whole lot better than I do, and I know now He'll hear and answer your prayer.

"Tell you what—I've never suggested this to anybody, but I'm going to pray that *God will be real to you in some way that you'll recognize!* I don't know what He'll do, but I believe He'll show you in some way that He hears you, and that you're getting through. Will you pray for the same thing?"

"I don't know how to pray, Boone—I really don't." He looked a little uneasy, suddenly aware of the unbelieving stares of the others.

"I don't mean right here, now," I said, "but later, when you're alone. You don't have any trouble talking to *me,* do you?"

Ace grinned, a little relieved, maybe. "No—but you're not God!"

"That's right, I'm not, and it's a good thing for you! But you can talk to Him just like you're talking to me. The words just don't matter, because He's listening to your heart anyway. You just need to keep in mind *who* you're talking to. It's important, though, that *you* speak to Him—and I will, too. Will you do it?"

"Okay. I'll try it, but—I don't know." He shook his head, and we walked out of the steam room.

On the way down to the hotel where I was working, I talked to the Lord out loud, "Dear Jesus, I don't know what I've gotten us into, but I really do pray for Ace. And I do pray right now that You'll show him—in *some way he'll recognize*—that You're listening to his prayer. Will you do it—please? Thank You, Lord."

It sounds good now, when I tell it, but I confess that my faith was pretty shaky. A Jew? A pornographer? A wild Las Vegas character— what *had* I gotten the Lord and me into? Or was it just me?

I prayed a lot for Ace the next two days.

I didn't see him, and I wasn't sure I wanted to.

But my engagement had come down to its final night, and for one last time, I went back to the Sands Health Club for a good steam and massage. I imagined I'd see Ace—and was sort of nervous about it.

He wasn't there; hardly anybody was. But while I was sitting in the steam room, the attendant pushed open the door to tell me I was wanted on the phone—a guy named Ace. As I went to pick up the receiver, I couldn't help wondering if I'd been set up for an elaborate joke, and this was the punch line.

The excitement on the other end of the line quickly erased the thought. "Your prayers are *answered!* **YOUR PRAYERS ARE ANSWERED!**" The voice was so loud I had to hold the phone away from my ear!

"Hold on, Ace," I squeezed the words in edgewise. "What's happened? What do you mean?"

"Boone! You know you said to just talk to God like I was talking to you? And to ask Him to show me something? Well, I thought you were probably crazy, but I did it. I mean, I talked right out loud, like you said. I really felt like I was talking to the lamp or the air, and I didn't think my words were gettin' outta the room—but I did it.

"And you must have been praying, too—right?"

I chuckled, "I sure was!"

"Well, *lemme tell you what happened!*

"I went in today for my last examination before the gall bladder operation. I was scared to death. The doc gave me this chalky stuff to drink and then X-rayed me. In a little while he came in with the X-rays and just shaking his head—he said he *couldn't find the stones!*

"*The gallstones are gone!*

"The doc says he can't operate on me when he can't find the stones!"

I was numb—I *really* was. "That's fantastic, Ace!"

"Yeah—but what do I do now?"

Again, I was just thunderstruck, practically speechless. I said the first thing that came to my mind, "Well, Ace, the main thing is—don't look at this as the end of anything; this is just the beginning!"

"Yeah . . . ?" He was eager. He wanted more.

"Why don't you get yourself a Bible, a modern language Bible that you can understand, and start reading about the One who's done this for you? It's obvious that He loves you, Ace. I'm amazed myself—but you know now that He's listening to you, don't you?"

I had more to say, but Ace interrupted, "Yeah. Yeah! I can dig it!" And he hung up!

He was running somewhere to get a Bible!

And there I sat, my mouth full of "Buts!" and "Waits!," my brain full of directions for him, my heart wanting to urge him into a Spirit-filled church fellowship—and my hand full of dead phone.

Slowly, as I sat there, beginning to wake up to what God had done, and to praise Him for responding so beautifully to our childish prayers, I saw what the Lord was showing *me* in this miracle!

He loved every last one of us—*equally*.

And *He knows which ones are ready to respond* to His miraculous touch. We don't. Jesus said there are so many people in the world who wouldn't believe if someone came back from the dead and stood before them! (*See* Luke 16:31.)

If all the people in Las Vegas had lined up for me to share and pray with, I'd have asked Ace to stand at the end of the line.

Jesus put him at the very front.

He did that with Zaccheus, didn't He?

Read Luke 19—and you'll see what I mean. I get choked up now when I see that little Jewish tax collector, a real oppressor of his own people on behalf of the Roman government, *called by name* while he crouched down in that tree, just hoping to see Jesus as He passed by.

He seemed like a foul little man, beneath contempt. But Jesus loved him, called him by name, and invited Himself to Zaccheus' house, bringing Him salvation. What a Lord!

And He did that for the adulterous woman (John 8:2–11), the thief on the cross (Luke 23:39–43)—and for me!

Now I just *start* to understand that hard thing Jesus said to His disciples, "No one can come to Me unless the Father who sent Me *draws him to Me*." (*See* John 6:44–66. Read it yourself, and think deep.)

You'll never come to the Father through Christ His Son, without experiencing a *miracle*, the supernatural touch of God in your life. Jesus says so!

Are you strongly attracted to this beautiful Person?

Does this Jesus seem to beckon you through the chaos and uncertainty of our crumbling world? Does He call you by name, in a still, small, insistent voice?

Then answer! Respond! It's a miracle! God Himself, in His gentle, loving concern for you, is cutting across the laws of nature and science —for you!

It's the most important miracle you'll ever experience. Don't shrug it off or rationalize it away. Just answer with a simple, "Yes, Lord." He'll take it from there.

I've never seen Ace again. He ran to get a Bible and I didn't get to tell him to be baptized, to ask for the Baptism in the Holy Spirit, what church to go to—or anything! Lord, You sure love him, don't You? Well, please don't let him get away.

And Ace, wherever you are—God loves you.

And you know it.

Matthew 9:10–13   Romans 5:8
2 Peter 3:9

7 THE OPEN DOOR

This may seem like a small thing—an insignificant thing—to some. But it's the kind of thing that happens to all of us, and I really think we should see the hand of God in it.

Is there such a thing as a "small miracle" anyway?

I'd been in my room in the Las Vegas hotel where I was working between shows. I was sharing my experience in Jesus with a young couple who'd driven over from northern California just to talk with me. They'd read *A New Song,* were attracted to this simple relationship with God I talked about, and had some questions to ask. They were from the same church background I was, and still were wrestling with some doctrinal hang-ups, or questions.

We talked for over two hours, had a great time, and wound up with a few minutes of refreshing prayer.

Then I looked at my watch—and my heart stopped! I was due *on stage,* dressed to sing, in four minutes! There was *no* way . . . .

I gulped apologies to the young couple, asked them to pray I'd make it somehow, and dashed from my room like a crazy man. Even as I ran down the hall, despair enveloped me—the elevators! They were always forever in coming; it was a popular, busy hotel, and even when one finally arrived, you could count on several stops before you got where you were going. I'd never make it. I was already starting to imagine the chaos this was going to cause.

"Please, Lord, please," I panted, just as I rounded the corner by the elevators.

An elevator stood open, empty—and waiting!

I jumped on as the door closed, pushed the button of the backstage floor and had a swift nonstop ride to that very floor, careened through the service passageways to my dressing room, and began to undress and dress at the same time! As clothes and shoes sailed all over the room, I kept repeating, "Praise the Lord! Praise the Lord!" between gulps of air.

Over the little monitor speaker in my dressing room I could hear the comedian finishing his act. For some reason, he seemed to be running *just a couple of minutes late.* The audience was really laughing, and had evidently slowed him down this particular show—out of sheer enjoyment. In my panic, it seemed they were laughing at me. And if they could have seen me, they would have been!

I zipped up, threw on my coat, ran backstage, and stepped into the wings just as the comedian, Jerry London, introduced me. My first two songs were sort of breathless, but I was even more keyed up than the audience, and the show went great. I was one grateful singer!

Now, why did I tell you this?

Surely I wouldn't call that a *miracle*. Would I?

If you'll check my definition of miracle, you'll see why I *do* call it just that. It *was* the touch of God in my life! I would never have made it if He hadn't intervened, and He knew it!

The Bible teaches me that my Father is interested in every detail of my life, and that "in my weakness His strength is perfected!" (*See* 2 Corinthians 12:9.) I believe it!

Why was that elevator waiting on the eleventh floor? Why? Why didn't it stop, even once, for somebody else? Why did the comedian "just happen" to be running long? You tell me. I think I know.

And why not thank the Lord instead of excusing it away to "luck"— or coincidence—or serendipity?

Romans 8:28   1 Corinthians 10:13

8   THE DEVIL IS A THIEF

The Devil loves to pick on kids.

You know that—don't you?

Well, he does. There's no OFF LIMITS, no neutral territory, no minimum age in this supernatural conflict we're in. If you still have doubts on that score, you don't have to go see *The Exorcist;* just read again Ephesians 6:10–13 and this from 1 Peter 5:8:

Be sober, be vigilant; because your adversary the devil, as a roaring lion, walketh about, seeking whom he may devour.

That's just about as clear as anybody could say it. And believe me, this adversary is not looking for a fight; he's looking first for defenseless people, and children are among his favorite targets!

So many of the fears and phobias and hang-ups and downright neuroses that afflict adults, Christians included, are the result of traumatic happenings that occurred when they were little, helpless children. Countless personalities have been warped by childhood tragedies, loneliness, frights, and diseases. Were these things brought about by God?

You know better.

I'm sure that's one of the big reasons Jesus stretched His hands to all the kids, wrapped His strong carpenter's arms around them, put them on His lap and said, "Suffer [permit] little children . . . to come unto me . . ." (Matthew 19:14). Sure, He loved them, more than we can imagine—but that's not all. Jesus knew they were in grave danger, and wanted to protect them Himself against unseen enemies.

That's why it's so important for *young kids to have their own personal encounters and experiences with Jesus.* They need to know their Big Brother—and where their strength really is.

Let me tell you what happened to Cherry.

This was several years ago, while she was still in high school.

We've never let the girls take any real money to school, just whatever they'd need for that day's activities. Obviously, we couldn't see any good reason to take more, and they might lose it. This was our rule.

But one day (for no good reason), Cherry took a ten dollar bill in her purse. Actually, it was her mother's purse which she'd borrowed for church the day before, and the money was in a special wallet inside. The wallet was special because it had been made by her granddaddy, Red Foley. Cherry had enjoyed carrying both those items to church, so the next day she took them to school with her.

She was in a hurry when she arrived, so she stuffed the purse in her locker and ran to class.

You know what happened, don't you? Right—when she opened her locker an hour later, the purse, wallet, and money were gone!

Cherry was really a wreck when she got home. Her mother's purse, her granddad's wallet—and her own ten dollars!—stolen. And all because of her own silly disobedience, which made it all even worse. She cried and cried.

"Daddy, who could have known? I mean, I know I was wrong to take the money to school, but I've never done it before—*who could have known* to go into *my* locker *this* particular day, and less than an hour after I got to school?"

I let her calm down a little, and then asked softly, "Who could have known, Cherry? Think about it a minute. Who is in a position to know that you're taking money to school—in disobedience, so you're not protected—just where it is, and when it'll be unguarded. And who is in a position to influence some other kid, who's spiritually weak and temptable, to open your locker just at the right time?"

Cherry sized it up immediately. "Can we pray about it, Daddy?"

You *know* my answer to that one!

And Shirley, who'd been quiet up till then, said, "Let's ask the Lord to return your wallet and my purse to you. He knows just where it is. And although you were wrong to take the money, the other things still belong to you, and the Lord gives us the right to ask for anything in His Name —okay?"

So we did.

Claiming the promises of Mark 11:24–26 (and incidentally, she forgave the culprit, in advance, according to that Scripture) and 1 John 5:14 and 15, we asked the Lord to cause Cherry's purse and wallet to be returned to her.

And they were!

Two days later, she was called to the school office, and there they were. They'd been found in a wooded area—without the ten dollars— and turned in.

Now, friend, unless you've had a similar experience with your own kids, you can't really appreciate what something like that does for your *own* faith, to say nothing of theirs!

For Cherry, it was a ten dollar lesson in what life is all about—and how good God and His Word are. She felt it was more than worth it.

The Psalmist David, a man after God's own heart, was still childlike in his response to the Lord when he wrote Psalms 56 and 59. You ought to read them.

And what was it the beloved Apostle John wrote?

Ye are of God, little children, and have overcome them: because greater is he that is in you, than he that is in the world.

1 John 4:4

9 ANGELS UNAWARE?

I'm in trouble now.

If I don't go ahead and tell you something about *each* of the girls— at least *one* of her own personal miracles—I'm doghouse-bound.

And you know what the Bible says: "Fathers, provoke not your children to anger, lest they be discouraged" (Colossians 3:21).

So here's one of Lindy's miracles.

Actually, the Miracle of the Mouse should qualify, but it was one of the early manifestations of God in our house, and it involved Laury, too. *And* the mouse!

Lindy's faith has grown steadily since then, and so has her knowledge of God's Word. Because of her intimate experience with Jesus, she knows she can take any problem to Him—and count on His answer!

So, over a year ago, when she developed a very sore throat and almost complete laryngitis, *right in the middle of our first singing summer,* she quietly began to talk to God about it.

The Boone Family had just begun a much-publicized engagement at the Playboy Hotel in Great Gorge, New Jersey. It seemed so strange to everybody that we'd be appearing in a Playboy place that *Time* magazine sent a reporter and photographer from New York City to do an article on it. You just may have read the account which quoted me as saying, ". . . I couldn't disagree more with the Playboy philosophy. But if Playboy wants to pay us to come here and present our *own* philosophy, we'll come."

And we did, to record-breaking crowds.

It was there, on our one night off, that I took the four daughters to dinner in the VIP room, the ultra-swank restaurant at the Playboy. Shirley was dieting, so she stayed in our rooms, eating celery. The lights were dim in the place, but the food was delicious, and while we were eating, a lady came over and identified herself as a long-time devoted fan and asked for an autograph. While I was signing her menu in the low light, she bent down and whispered, "What's your wife going to think about this?"

I looked up. "Think about what?"

"About your having dinner with four Bunnies . . ." she said with a slight nod toward my girls. She was serious!

"Ma'am," I answered, "these aren't Bunnies. They're Boonies!"

We laughed our heads off at that, but when Lindy came down with her throat problem a couple of days later, it was time to be serious. *Real* serious. Because once you team up as a family, and build your whole performance around the family—if *one* of you is sick, you *all* are!

So, early in the afternoon, when we saw that Lindy could hardly make a sound, we prayed earnestly, and called a doctor. While we were waiting for him to come, we prayed some more. I was about to anoint her with oil, according to James 5:13–16, when there was a knock at the door.

Assuming it was the doctor, I put the oil away for a few minutes and answered the knock. But instead of Marcus Welby and his black bag, I was confronted by two young "hippie"-looking guys! Their hair hung past their shoulders, their jeans spoke eloquently of years gone by, and their feet were barely thonged with worn-down sandals.

"Can we talk to you for a moment, Mr. Boone?" one asked gently.

"I'm sorry, guys," I said, "but I really can't talk right now. My daughter is sick and I thought you were the doctor . . . ." I was about to suggest they come back some other time, when the fellow interrupted.

"We know. That's why we're here. The Lord told us to come." And they both smiled.

I don't mind telling you I was confused. Had the doctor sent them? No; they really hadn't known what the reason was, but they had been praying in a nearby town when they felt definitely impressed by the Lord to come find us and pray with us, I had just given them the reason—and here they were!

While I was still standing in the doorway (trying to grasp all of this), the doctor arrived.

He went in to Lindy, diagnosed the case as severe bronchitis, prescribed a heavy antibiotic, and left, assuring us that Lindy would not be able to sing—or even talk, probably—for several days!

Now normally we'd have been almost panicked. Without Lindy, we really didn't have a show, and both shows for that evening and the next were sold out! But here stood these two young strangers—and I had a strong feeling "something was up."

Even the way they got past the really strict security guards around the hotel was an amazing story, with a suspiciously supernatural ring to it, but I'll tell you that some other time. I invited them in, and in a moment, they had joined Shirley and me at Lindy's bed, I anointed her forehead with oil, reading the passage from James—and together we prayed and praised the Lord.

We visited for a few minutes more, and the boys left.

The prescribed medicine came, Lindy took the first couple of pills and went to sleep until dinner time.

When the room-service dinner came, we woke her up. While we ate, she began to speak softly, and afterwards she hummed a little to sort of warm-up. By show time she was smiling that big beamer of hers and assuring us she was going to be fine—she'd make it.

You know the rest, don't you?

Right—almost!

She sang very well, felt almost "up to snuff," and carried her part of the program beautifully, except for a couple of frightening moments which the audiences never knew about. Lindy said later that twice, when she heard her own voice singing strong and true—when the doctor had said just hours before it was impossible—she started to cry!

That would have ruined the whole thing!

So she quickly prayed in the Spirit, within herself, and regained control. She had to force herself to forget, momentarily, that she was *right in the middle of a miracle*. And the show went on.

We were a happy bunch when that day ended, and the Boone family told the Lord so, with much praise and thanksgiving.

Let brotherly love continue. Be not forgetful to entertain strangers: for thereby some have entertained angels unawares.

Hebrews 13:1, 2

I don't really think those two young men were angels—but I surely don't doubt that our loving Father arranged for them to show up at our door when they did, to participate in Lindy's miracle. He's done it before, lots of times!

I love the Lord, because he hath heard my voice and my supplications.

Psalms 116:1

Genesis 19   Acts 23:12–31
Acts 8:26–39   Hebrews 13:8
Luke 24:13–35

10   DEBBY'S MIRACLE

Lots of wonderful things have happened to our little blonde, Debby, in the last several years (as they have to each of us), but I have my reasons for wanting to tell this one.

First, Debby has always hated school. Well, maybe not "hated"—but she *has* always liked early morning, evenings, weekends, and eggplant better. It's not surprising, then, that she hasn't always been an *A* student. There always seemed to have been personality conflicts with her teachers, more homework than she could quite handle, and interruptions like sickness, travel, and other duties (like church attendance) that always kept her behind in assignments.

She says her ultimate dream has always been to just get out of school —forever.

Second, she hates pressure—and seldom performs well in a pressure situation. She's pretty thorough in her responsibility, especially when it's something she likes and is interested in; but to be faced with a "test" of some kind, especially when she doesn't feel ready for it, is sure to throw her into a tailspin of raw nerves, tears, self-doubt and blotch-neck.

That's why I know this was a miracle.

We'd been touring Japan, the family and I, on a singing concert tour. In fact, this particular tour, our second as a family, took us all over the Orient, from the major cities of Japan to Hong Kong, Seoul, Taiwan, Singapore, Manila and Bangkok. It was fantastic, both as an experience for our family and as a commercial success.

We all thought it was such a great opportunity that we decided the girls could miss a couple of weeks of school to do it. The teachers agreed, and had given each of them advance assignments that should keep them up with their classes while they were gone. So, in addition to the regular baggage (and our gang has a ton of it!), we had to lug all their school books and study material along, too.

Can you imagine the agony?

Picture yourself in all those romantic, exotic Far Eastern capitals, wanting to see everything, go everywhere, eat all the local foods, and learn at least a few words of the native language; having to sing almost every night, in a different country; and then, on planes and backstage and in your hotel rooms—having to study "new math"!

It was rough.

But the girls did it, and with surprising good spirits, too. Fortunately, the girls like to learn (with the possible exception of Deb), and they really pitch in and help each other with their individual weak spots. It really made me proud to see them settle on a plane, after a couple of exciting days in Bangkok: floating down the *klongs* (or inland waterways), meeting royalty, and the reigning Miss Universe (herself a Thai) —and watch them haul out their grammar and history books and really "chop wood"!

Debby, as I remember, was especially diligent, not wanting to start back to school hopelessly behind the eight ball. She'd had enough of that. Once in a while along the way, I tried to help her with some knotty problem; but mostly, she studied and did her work on her own.

So, when we got home, I felt she'd be right up with her class and ready for anything.

Characteristically, she didn't feel that way.

The day we got home, she called her best friend and found out there was a math test the next day! She started to go to pieces.

She said, "Daddy, I *can't* take that test. I'm not ready. I know I'll flunk it—will you write my teacher a note, so I can take it later?"

Well, I've never minded doing that—when I felt it was called for. But in this case, I knew Debby had been studying, and imagined she was really capable of doing well on the test, *if* she went in with an optimistic attitude. Besides, the school had already bent over backwards to let us be gone that long—and I hated to ask for any more favors. I really felt Deb should go on and take the test, sink or swim—and I told her so.

Just a little more background is called for. We'd prayed a lot along the way, had enjoyed some intense spiritual experiences in family worship and in sharing times with Christians in almost every country we'd visited, and had a keen sense of the Lord's guidance and protection and loving care throughout the whole trip!

It didn't seem right, somehow, to have counted on the Lord so heavily *outside* the United States—and then to behave as if we'd left Him in customs coming home!

So, in spite of her tears and honest feeling of inadequacy, I finally said, "Honey, let's pray. I know you've crammed your pretty head with the right facts and know-how. All you need is to relax and approach this test with confidence. That's just another word for *faith,* isn't it? Hasn't the Lord shown us His power and provision while we were gone? Don't you think He's interested in helping you with your responsibilities here, too? Let's pray that He'll give you peace tomorrow and remind you of all the math you've actually learned while you were on the trip—and Mommy and I will be happy with whatever grade you make, as long as you do your best. Okay?"

It was like agreeing to her own doom, but Deb sighed and said, "Okay." We prayed earnestly together, and I made her go on to bed without even staying up late to study! I felt she needed rest more than anything.

Then Shirley and I prayed some more after she'd gone to sleep.

The next night at dinner, I asked Deb how she'd done; she said she really didn't know, that she *thought* she'd handled the test all right, but that she'd thought that lots of other times before, only to find out she hadn't. She seemed so relieved just to have it behind her, and was glad that we hadn't put it off. So she *did* have peace—and the grade we'd have to wait for.

A couple of days went by and I almost forgot about it. Then I arrived home just in time for dinner, and the first thing I saw was Deb's long face!

"Daddy . . ." she said hesitantly, "you know the test you made me take? You wouldn't let me put it off, even though I *told* you I wasn't ready? All we did was pray . . . ?"

I nodded, feeling a little dread rising in me. "What happened?"

She took a paper from behind her back and held it toward me. In the upper righthand corner was a big fat red *A!*

Well, we laughed and whooped and hugged, and laughed some more. Then, right in the middle of our thanks for the meal, we all thanked God for His confirmation that He wasn't just our Road Manager! He was still living in our house, and going to school with the girls every day!

And since that evening—Debby has become a straight *A* student.

She'd always had the ability but she'd doubted it. Once she *knew* she had a Partner, a spiritual Tutor who would help her achieve her own full potential, she's been a different kind of student. She actually likes her teachers—and herself—a lot more.

What does Paul assure us?

There hath no temptation [test] taken you but such as is common to man: *but God is faithful, who will not suffer [allow] you to be tempted [tested] above that ye are able;* but will with the temptation [test] also make a way to escape, that *ye may be able to bear it.*

See 1 Corinthians 10:13

And James?

Dear brothers, is your life full of difficulties and temptations? Then be happy, for when the way is rough, *your patience has a chance to grow.* So let it grow, and don't try to squirm out of your problems.

James 1:2, 3 (LB)

Paul again:

Be [anxious in] nothing; but in every thing by prayer and supplication with thanksgiving let your requests be made known unto God. And the peace of God which passeth all understanding, shall keep your hearts *and minds* through Christ Jesus. . . . I can do all things through Christ which strengtheneth me.

See Philippians 4:6, 7, 13

Let me tell you, when you experience the reality of these words in *test* situations, they mean a whole lot more to you!

We praise Jesus for what He showed Debby—and her parents.

11   LAURY TAKES A DIVE

Onstage, in Ogden, Utah, fourteen-year-old Laury passed out cold—right in the middle of a song!

Just keeled over backwards and hit the stage with a thump! (accompanied by gasps from the audience of some six thousand). We, the whole family and I, were nearing the end of our performance, singing our "Foley Medley," a collection of our favorite Red Foley songs. I think it was during "Steal Away"—that Laury did!

Ernie Retino, one of our singers, bent down and gathered Laury up and hurried off-stage with her (that's not as easy as it sounds, but he did it—pronto). Sort of numb, but conditioned through years of coping with the unexpected, I led the family through the rest of that number, assured the audience that Laury was fine, and hustled right into our closer.

Although that audience was one of the warmest, most enthusiastic we ever had, we couldn't wait to take our bows and get off. Shirley, as as you might imagine, was frantic to know what was wrong with Laury, and so were all of us.

We found her on a cot in the girls' dressing room, with Ernie and a nurse looking after her. She was conscious, a little dazed, but not much the worse for the fall; she was embarrassed beyond words, though, that she had inadvertently disrupted our show, and right at the end, at that. We couldn't have cared less about *that* right then; we wanted to know what had happened? Why?

Laury didn't know.

All she could remember was that she had suddenly gotten very dizzy, that a powerful wave of nausea and light-headedness had swept over her —and that, no matter how she fought it, she just seemed unable to resist it. She could barely remember the first of the Foley hymns—and then looking up into Ernie's face backstage. It was all very peculiar.

The whole family joined hands around her as she sat on the edge of the cot, and we prayed for her. We prayed, not just for her restored health and well-being, but to *bind Satan* and his intentions in this situation, whatever they were.

Almost by the time we said, "Amen," Laury was fine!

There was no recurrence, no indication that anything was wrong, no upset stomach or flu or headache, no further symptoms or trace of any physical cause. We still don't know, for sure, what caused her to pass out that way.

But I have an idea.

More than an idea: a strong conviction.

Laury confessed something to me that night, just before we had our good-night prayer session together. She had been reading a book on astrology that afternoon, on our bus. She knew that our family is strongly opposed to any contact with the occult, and that we had openly discussed astrology as the world's oldest "anti-God" religion. (If that comes as a surprise to you, check the end of this story.) But one of our musicians (who's no longer with us) had brought the book on the bus with him, and inquisitive, impulsive, and slightly headstrong Laury had sneaked a half-hour, satisfying her curiosity.

Not only that, but she had also imitated this particular musician in assuming a lotus position and "meditating"—withdrawing within one-self and allowing the consciousness to seek "a deeper, more tranquil and liberated level"—for another half hour!

Now, friend—you may be shocked to read that these things bothered me. And to be truthful, I wouldn't have been as bothered *before* the fact as after! If I'd seen Laury reading that book on the bus, I would probably have rather calmly taken it away from her, given it back to the musician with a request to keep it to himself, and sat down for a long chat with my daughter about the dangers of "messing" with something that God condemns.

I certainly wouldn't have tried "scare tactics," warning Laury that if she opened her mind to these things (that most people consider helpful or harmless) some terrible thing might happen to her. I would have taken a more moderate approach.

I think that's why the Lord let Laury take a dive.

I believe *He* saw more danger to her in what she was doing than I did!

And therefore He permitted a shocking demonstration of where dis-obedience and dabbling in the occult can lead. Laury seems more sensi-tive to suggestion than our other daughters, and this is good and bad: good when she's sensitive to the Lord and the "right" of a situation; but very bad when she allows herself to be influenced by wayward friends and her own fleshly appetites. Under the guidance of the Holy Spirit, Laury has "prophesied" in our family prayer times—that is, uttered knowledge and admonition that are beyond her human capability—but she has also demonstrated a vulnerability to the whisperings of Satan.

By that, I mean she has surprisingly and rather easily been drawn into temptation, into things she knows are wrong and will regret later, both with friends and alone. She tends to be impulsive, impetuous, and a little erratic.

Like Peter, the apostle.

In chapter 16 of Matthew, there's the startling example of Peter's susceptibility to influence, both God's and Satan's. First, Jesus commended him for *receiving directly from God* the revelation that Jesus was "the Christ, the Son of the Living God"; but then—less than ten verses later—Jesus rebuked him for "savoring the things of men, and not of God," and for being directly influenced *by Satan!* (*See* v. 23.)

Peter, too, was impulsive, impetuous, and a little erratic.

God could use a dynamic, impulsive man like Peter—and so could the Devil.

I believe each of our kids is caught in the middle of a spiritual tug-of-war; and that goes for yours, too. God has a plan for each life; and Satan intends to foul that up in any way he can, and the sooner the better. He has no scruples about infecting the mind of the young, about possessing the spirits (if he can) of children, of traumatizing even babies and very little kids and twisting their perceptions of spiritual reality. If he can "get them" while they're young—they're not likely to give him any trouble when they're older. He's no dummy, this Satanic Majesty, and an innocent, cherubic baby girl is like a disease-infested cockroach to him—a threat to his very existence and earthly power. (Please read Luke 9:37–42.)

Didn't Jesus say that *He came to make each of us like trusting, harmless little children* (*see* Matthew 18:3)—and we would eventually, in our childlike state, be the *very instruments of Satan's destruction* (*see* Revelation 12:9–11)?

We're in a daily battle, a battle to the death, my friend—and it involves your children and mine, as well as ourselves. We'd better face it and arm ourselves and prepare our kids to recognize the Enemy when he approaches them with his enticements and his wily, tantalizing bag of tricks—as he surely does.

Jesus referred to His disciples as His "children"—and He warned Peter that Satan had asked to "sift him like wheat," to really work him over (*see* Luke 22:31). Jesus said He was simply praying for Peter, that after he came through the tests and trials and "falling on his face," his faith would not have failed—but have made him stronger. And that's the way it worked out!

I really believe the Lord Jesus allowed Laury to be "sifted" a little that day in Ogden—and that she's much stronger now because of it. She's not nearly as tempted to flirt with forbidden things. She *knows*, firsthand, who's dangling that appealing counterfeit in front of her, and what it can do to her!

Oh yes . . . if you want to know God's attitude toward disobedience (kids' and otherwise) and occult substitutes like astrology and transcendental meditation (whose real gurus say can eventually lift you to God-Oneness by your own effort), check these Scriptures.

Deuteronomy 21:18–21	Ephesians 6:1–4	Isaiah 14:12–17
Deuteronomy 18:9–14	Isaiah 47:9–15	Galatians 1:8, 9
Deuteronomy 17:2–7	1 Samuel 15:23	Psalms 1:1, 2
	1 Timothy 4:15, 16	
	Philippians 4:6–8	

12   MIRACLE OF THE FLY

I've told elsewhere the Miracle of the Oaks: the $2 million "Red-Sea experience"—how, after being told by my own advisors *on Wednesday* I'd be bankrupt by week's end, a man flew from Washintgon, D.C., to San Francisco with almost $2 million and bought the Oakland Oaks pro-basketball team *on Friday!* None of us knew this man existed, and

I have yet to meet him. Although, operating in his own interests, he became my own "Moses," rescuing me from personal disaster—I still don't know what he looks like!

And yet, because of what happened *on Thursday* of that same week, I knew that my deliverance was at hand, and confidently said so.

I call it the Miracle of the Fly.

It was a sweltering, still, August noon, and it seemed to me that even Nature was holding its hot breath in anticipation, knowing God was about to do something spectacular for this bumbling singer.

Since there was absolutely nothing I could do anymore to solve my own dilemma with the Oaks, and since my own lawyers and advisors had sadly given up the fight, I was just standing in the shallow end of our Beverly Hills swimming pool, waist-deep, waiting and wading and occasionally telling the Lord I loved Him and trusted Him to save me.

The sun had that Southern California bake-oven quality, and the static stifling heat helped create an unreal sort of vacuum feeling. I remember closing my eyes in prayer for quite some time—and when I opened them, the first thing I saw was a fly, floating on the still surface of the water, fluttering and floundering, trying futilely to fly out of this strange predicament!

My idle thought was, "It's had it . . ." and I looked away, returning to prayer. Who cared about a fly, anyway?

I looked back.

The despised little thing was still putting up a valiant fight, making lots of little ripples, determined in some way to get a foothold, some kind of leverage somewhere, before it was too late. But it was out in the middle of a vast pool, and there was absolutely no hope. Perhaps if it could see things from my vantage point, it would recognize how silly it was to fight—and just give up and drown. I watched its struggle with only partial interest.

And then—I began to identify with the little creature!

After all, wasn't I just like him? Wasn't I trapped in an incomprehensible circumstance, fighting and hoping against all odds for my very existence? What if God was watching *me*, in sort of amused detachment, waiting for me to give up and drown?

I suddenly wanted that fly to live.

I cupped my hands, reached down beneath it in the water, and slowly raised them letting the water drain through my fingers until just the fly remained on my left hand, weaker but still struggling. I waded over to the side and deposited the little thing on the concrete to dry. For a few minutes it sat in its own fast-evaporating puddle, stretching and drying its wings—and then, abruptly, flew away.

I thought about it for a while, and then began to really praise the Lord.

"My Father," I cried, raising my hands skyward, "thank You for showing me that. If I can save that fly from *its* troubles—you can sure save me from mine. And I believe You will, Lord, now more than ever! Thank You, thank You!"

I know, it may seem foolish to you, but in my heart I *knew* that God cared a lot more about me than I did about a fly—and if I felt sudden pity for a tiny creature like that insect, the fantastic heart of Almighty Jehovah must feel *my* need, and must already be reaching toward me with cupped hands, to lift me from certain disaster. How can I tell you? I knew it!

There was one major, fantastic difference between my situation and the fly's.

The fly would never be able to understand what had happened to it.

All it could possibly know is that it was in some kind of terrible trouble—and now it wasn't. No way could it ever comprehend me, or the nature of its own difficulty, or why it was flying again, safe and sound.

As I stood there in the water, it hit me that *only if I became a fly* could I ever communicate to it, in its own terms, what its terrible fatal danger was, and how it had been rescued.

How I loved Jesus in that moment.

Because that's what He did.

He became a man.

And He did it to show us God in man's terms, and so that God could feel what man feels. He did it to show us our fatal human condition, and to provide, Himself, the rescue.

He showed us God's own outstretched hands. His very Name, *Yeho-shua* in Hebrew means JEHOVAH IS SALVATION!

But it cost Him His life. The other flies killed Him for His trouble. And though He knew ahead of time this would happen, He came anyway!

He loved us that much—John 3:16.

"Well, all right . . . ," you may be saying, "but that was no *miracle* —what you did for the fly. Anybody could've done what you did!"

And you're right. My rescuing the fly wasn't a miracle, although I believe God arranged that happening to show me something and bolster my faith (because my $2 million miracle *did* happen the next day!). But maybe you're looking at this miracle from the wrong angle.

Put yourself in the fly's place.

For when we were yet without strength, in due time Christ died for the ungodly. For scarcely for a righteous man will one die: yet peradventure [perhaps] for a good man some would even dare to die. But God commendeth his love toward us, in that, while we were yet sinners, Christ died for us. Much more then, being now justified by his blood, we shall be saved from wrath through him. For if, when we were enemies, we were reconciled to God by the death of his Son, much more, being reconciled, we shall be saved by his life.

And not only so, but we also joy in God through our Lord Jesus Christ, by whom we have now received the atonement.

Romans 5:6–11

Romans 5:1–21	Matthew 21:33–46
Matthew 21:17–22	1 Corinthians 10:13

13   MONEY MIRACLE NUMBER ONE

I want to tell you about a couple of financial miracles.

Some people can imagine God getting involved in almost any part of our lives—except our finances. What does He know—or care—about money, anyway? Oh, that's right; we *are* supposed to give (it's called tithing, isn't it?)—so the Lord knows something about *receiving* money. But does He really concern Himself with our financial needs; is He ever on the *giving* end of money matters?

Oh, *yes*—He is!

My friend, Cal Habern, a businessman in Dallas, can tell you firsthand.

Cal read an article in *Christian Life* magazine one day. A friend had given it to him, hoping to interest Cal in giving his own life to the Lord. Cal was a tremendously successful businessman, involved in electronics and manufacturing in Denver and Dallas. He was a nominal Episcopalian, an occasional churchgoer, and all-round good guy. But he didn't know Jesus, at least not as Lord of his life.

The friend hoped that the article, which happened to be about Harald Bredesen (a Christian Reformed minister), Dean Dennis (a Church of Christ minister), and me, and our varied but exciting experiences with the Holy Spirit, would intrigue Cal. It did.

Soon, he came to Los Angeles on business, and arranged through a mutual friend to meet me. Shirl and I had him over for dinner, fell in love with him, shared our whole testimony with him, took him to church with us, and included him in a couple of dramatic answers to prayer that came through while he was here. He gave his life to Jesus, called his wife, Peggy, to tell her—and called his business associates to announce their company had a new chairman of the board: the Lord!

That's the kind of guy Cal is—all-out, total, get-on-with-it! Oh, he didn't mean they were going to put Jesus' Name on the stationery or the corporate office doors; he just meant that Cal Habern was turning over his companies to the Lord's oversight and direction.

And the Lord took him up on it!

At first, it appeared the bottom had fallen out of everything: difficulties arose, subsidiaries had to be jettisoned, there was a wholesale reshuffling of personnel and priorities, and over a period of several months, Cal's faith had to grow fast and deep to meet the challenges. He even wondered sometimes if he shouldn't have just left well enough alone and remained a successful, self-satisfied businessman.

But after those first few hectic months of his new life, he looked back and took stock. He saw that his business life had taken a solid, exciting new direction, and that all of the things that the Lord had weeded out of his life and corporate interests were the troublemakers and potential disasters! He was in *better* shape than before. And in addition, an ailing marriage was welded together for keeps; his relationships with his kids had solidified; and his new walk with Jesus had made a real *man* of him, in every important and lasting way.

All this sets the stage for Money Miracle Number 1.

Cal was facing a $110,000 deadline—personally. He had to have that sum, and there was no apparent place to get it. He needed the money immediately to wind up his last sticky obligation since he'd made the Lord his Chairman. But there wasn't a clue as to how to get it! And it was urgent!

So he and his wife Peggy did the businesslike thing: they prayed.

And as they prayed, the Lord seemed to impress on them Mark 11:24, "Therefore I say unto you, What things soever ye desire, when ye pray, believe that ye receive them, and ye shall have them." Cal asked himself, "If I really believe I have what I'm asking for, how should I act? I mean, if Jesus walked in here and handed me $110, 000—what would I do?"

He and Peggy decided that the first thing they would do is give a tenth of that amount back to the Lord, in gratitude.

So they decided to thank the Lord in advance—and give him $11,000!

By scraping together everything they had that wasn't nailed down, they raised that amount, and presented the check to a dynamic evangelist, Kenneth Copeland—who just *happened* to be facing a need in his fast-growing ministry for that exact amount! And they all prayed together, praising the Lord for His goodness in meeting both Ken's need—and the Haberns'.

In just days (and within the deadline period), Cal's money emerged: in the hands of businessmen who for their own reasons wanted to invest in Cal's ongoing business. It was amazing! With no effort on his own part, he added up $101,000 in new business capital that could take care of his obligation and springboard him in his new venture. But wait! He was still $9,000 short.

Out of the blue, a new man walked into his life and presented Cal with an envelope, saying he wanted to be in business with Cal. Before he opened the envelope, Cal knew what he'd see—and he was right.

A check for $9,000.

Now I don't know how this story affects you. But it makes me want to praise the Lord! And I know how it affected Cal and Peggy Habern —they have become—increasingly—glowing exhibits of Jesus' love, deeply dedicated disciples and wise stewards in His service.

And if you're uncertain about God's *desire* to bless you materially and be involved with you financially, check these Scriptures, just for a start: Mark 10:28–31, Luke 6:38, and 2 Corinthians 8 and 9, especially 9:6–15. He *wants* to trust us with abundance!

> Now unto him that is able to do exceeding abundantly above all that we ask or think, according to the power that worketh in us, Unto him be glory in the church by Christ Jesus throughout all ages, world without end. Amen.
>
> Ephesians 3:20, 21

Amen!

14 MONEY MIRACLE NUMBER TWO

This story involves Cal Habern, too.

For His own good reasons, the Lord seems to have given Cal a "money ministry," raising and handling money and business ventures, especially those in which there is some big consequence to the Kingdom. Cal especially looks for things that will somehow help the Body of Christ and "get the Word out," in modern, efficient, businesslike ways. He often has to put the project together from the beginning—and that means raising the money!

And although he was educated as a businessman, when he turned his life over to Jesus, the Lord had to put him through a graduate course!

Cal and I both have been puzzled and challenged by the Lord's sad observation, ". . . for the children of this world are in their generation *wiser than the children of light*" (*see* Luke 16:8). In the midst of a story that seems to commend an unjust steward for at least a practical, realistic approach to his problems and goals, Jesus says that He wishes we would learn how to properly handle material things, so that He could trust us with far greater *spiritual* riches. (*See* verses 11, 12.)

As part of his new education, Cal faced another deadline.

This time the cash need was $114,000. Habern had organized a new TV production company, Trans-American Video, Inc., in Hollywood. The firm (one of the largest television production and marketing companies in the world) was formed as a secular organization run by Christians for both Christian and secular productions. It grieved him, as a citizen and a father, to see what was happening to commercial TV, and typically, he jumped in to try to change the situation. He decided that a first-class production company, offering the highest quality facilities and management in the industry, could make a real impact on the kinds of programming coming out of Hollywood. Especially with Christians in all the key positions!

So he set about to do it. He got the initial money, found the right people, acquired facilities, and set to work. He went to Germany to personally purchase the latest TV cameras (better than anything we had yet in this country)—and on the strength of these early moves TAV landed a contract with CBS to cover all their live sports events!

But right after the cameras were put to work a cash crunch developed. Cal learned on a Friday that unless he could hand over to the camera company $114,000 by Monday morning—he would lose the cameras *and* his company!

There was just no way, at least that Cal could see, so he and Peggy retired to the "executive suite"—their prayer room—and turned it over to their Chairman of the Board. In prayer, Peggy received a definite instruction from the Lord that He would handle it, and that *Cal was to call no one;* they were to be ". . . still, and see the salvation of the Lord" (2 Chronicles 20:17). It frightened them; it was definitely against Cal's own do-it-yourself nature, but they decided to obey.

It was now late Friday afternoon, too late for any business, so Cal went out to mow his lawn, leaving the door open slightly, so that he could hear the phone ring.

It did.

Cal answered and heard the voice of Wallace Johnson, vice chairman of the board of Holiday Inns. "Hello, Cal—this is Wallace Johnson. I'm returning your call."

Cal was numb. He hadn't called Mr. Johnson!

Oh, he had several weeks before; but the reason for that call had long since passed, and Cal couldn't even remember why he'd tried to reach this well-known Christian businessman.

So they chatted for a few minutes, and then Cal told Wallace Johnson of his own urgent problem. "You need $114,000 cash *by Monday?*" Wallace said. "There's no way I can personally help you now." But Cal knew that Mr. Johnson was a vital link in this miracle, and asked him to believe with him, which he did. After a moment or so in silent prayer, Wallace suggested that Clement Stone, in Chicago (another renowned Christian businessman and founder of Combined Insurance Companies of America) might be able to help—and just might be really interested in Trans-American Video and its goals.

Wallace phoned Mr. Stone, put him in touch with Cal; Saturday Cal flew to Chicago to meet with Clement Stone and his advisors at his home —and in a matter of hours, Cal Habern and W. Clement Stone were partners!

Today, as you can imagine, TAV is a going, growing concern, with Christians at the top, and a fantastic opportunity to make inroads in television, where 200 million people gather every day! Now if this story were just an account of how the Lord took a hand in a man's business affairs, it would still thrill me; for God says in Proverbs 16:3, "Commit thy works unto the Lord, and thy thoughts shall be established"— and He means it!

But there's more to this particular miracle than that.

In Matthew 20:30-34, Jesus is stopped by two blind men, crying for sight; "So Jesus had compassion on them, and touched their eyes: and immediately their eyes received sight, and they followed Him" (v. 34).

In Romans 10:16 the Prophet Isaiah is pictured crying, "Lord, who hath believed our report?" And Paul answers, prophetically in part, "So then faith cometh by hearing, and hearing by the word of God. But I say, Have they not heard? Yes verily, their sound went *into all the earth, and their words unto the ends of the world*" (*see* vs. 17, 18).

How can that happen in this jet age? How can over 3 billion hear, and see, the Good News of Jesus in our generation?

God has a plan. He'll get it done.

And I think Cal Habern has a part in that plan.

I hope you and I do, too.

15   GOOSE BUMPS GALORE

"Please pray for us—the fires are all around us, the whole area has been evacuated, and Gary's still out at our house, determined to fight it with our garden hose until it's hopeless!"

We were at Sunday school, and the request came from a longtime friend of Shirley's and mine. Angela's voice and face showed the strain of anguish and sleeplessness—and concern for her husband, Gary. Their new home was right in the path of one of those raging fires that flare up every so often in the hills surrounding Los Angeles. The L.A. fire-fighting teams had so far had very little success in containing the latest holocaust, whipped and driven by what the papers were calling "devil winds."

Of course, our class joined in prayer for Gary, Angela, and their home. On our way home after church, the family and I prayed again, claiming God's protection and rebuking the work of Satan in Jesus' Name. We wondered out loud if anybody in the press realized how accurate the term "devil winds" probably was!

We checked TV and radio for the latest reports on the fire—and then it hit me that I could probably call Gary and find out; wasn't he right out there in the eye of the storm? I dialed the number.

Busy.

I dialed again.

Busy.

Who could Gary be talking to? I dialed again. *Busy, busy, busy.*

I checked with the operator—and she explained that the busy signal was because the lines were down! There was nothing going in or out of that area now, because of the fire!

Now I was frustrated, and more than a little anxious for Gary myself.

So I prayed, "Lord, the operator says I can't get through. But I'm going to try one more time. If it's just Satan hindering my getting through to Gary, I rebuke him in Jesus' Name. Help me, Lord. Thank You, Jesus . . ." as I dialed one last time.

It rang!

When Gary answered, I asked him, "What's happening out there, brother?"

"Oh, I'm just sitting here watching the fire—it's pretty close, now," he answered, not sounding overly worried about it.

I told him about my trouble getting through to him, and my prayer, and how the phone had rung immediately after my request of the Lord.

"Now stop that, Boone—you're giving me goose bumps!"

Gary had a little trouble, like most of us these days, believing that the Lord would take that direct a hand in our concerns. And yet he knew that I and my family had received some wonderful answers to our prayers.

I assured him that what I'd told him was true, and that our class at Sunday school had prayed for him and his house, and that the Boones were warring in prayer for him. I asked him, almost as an afterthought, "*You're* praying about it, aren't you, Gary?"

There was sort of a pause on the other end of the line.

Then Gary, in his truly humble way, said he felt the Lord had more important things to do than just watch over his house—and that he was really sort of reluctant to "bother Him" about it! And so many folks today feel just that way!

"Listen, Gary," I jumped in, "are you a Christian?"

He assured me he was.

"Then you belong to Jesus, *right?*" Again, he agreed. "Then everything you *have* belongs to Him, doesn't it?" He said he guessed that was so.

"Well, then—will you ask Jesus to protect *His own property,* for Pete's sake?"

I felt sort of a breakthrough; Gary chuckled and said he hadn't thought of it that way before, and that he would start praying right away.

I went on to tell him how the Bible describes Satan as "the prince of the power of the air" (Ephesians 2:2), and that if I were out there with him, we would walk over the whole perimeter of his property and claim it in Jesus' Name and forbid that wicked prince to touch it. I could tell that was a little heavy for Gary, so I just assured him that we would be doing that for him, through prayer.

He thanked me and the family, we chatted just a moment more, and then we hung up. Then Shirley and I really went to war in prayer.

I left town the next day, and it was several days before I heard what happened. The fires raged all around that area the rest of Sunday, destroying homes and property on three sides of Gary's house—but *left his home and land completely untouched!*

I saw him at church the next Sunday, and as I walked up to him he had a curious smile on his face, both jubilant and cautious. I was bubbling over with joy, and I said, "God's good, isn't He?"

Gary laughed, "Now watch it, Boone—you're giving me goose bumps again!"

Ah, what wonderful goose bumps! Have you ever wondered about that little phenomenon, anyway? Where they come from—what causes them? I've never heard a scientific explanation; I'm not sure there is one. But I do know one thing: They seem related to spiritual things.

You always seem to get goosebumpy when you hear about some wonderful or terrible or unexplainable thing—and the actual physical manifestation of "goose flesh" is really not related to an intellectual process, or even always an emotional one. So often, the feeling and its visible manifestation spring from a *spiritual* reaction in the deep inner being. Like fur rising on a cat's back, it seems to be an instinct. Could our spirits be trying to tell us something?

Anyway, like Gary, *I* get goose bumps when I sense that the living God has put His fatherly finger into the course of human events—and touched my life, or the lives of people around me.

I *know* He heard our prayer that day, and "put a hedge around" Gary's home to protect it, just as He did for Job (Job 1:10). I think He wanted those dear people to realize He is present—*Jehovah shammah*

(*The Lord is there,* in Hebrew)—and that, too often, we "have not, because we *ask not*" (*see* James 4:2).

Oh, if we would only take literally Jesus' promise to be "with you always, even unto the end of the world" (*see* Matthew 28:20). If we would only meditate a little bit on His invitation to ask *anything* in His Name, and then to believe! (*See* Mark 11:24.) If it would only strike us with full force that Jesus promised to *manifest Himself*—to demonstrate His Presence—to anyone who endeavors to keep His commandments! (*See* John 14:21.)

Why, we'd soon be experiencing a *miracle a day!*

Complete with goose bumps!

16   OVER THE CLIFF IN A VOLKSWAGEN

Just for a minute, ask yourself what might run through your mind as you start over a precipice at the beginning of a 700-foot drop to the rocks below—in a Volkswagen.

See the spray rising from the Bermuda rocks as the waves dash against them, scattering sun-diamonds in the breeze; see the turquoise sea stretching placidly to the horizon, as if backing away from the tragedy about to shatter you and your world into oblivion; see yourself, in the little car, dreamlike in slow motion, gripping the wheel as you leave the gravel surface, bounce over the hard-earth edge of the mountainside, and drift out onto nothing, the ocean tilting crazily as the hood of the VW noses toward the beckoning rocks below.

What do you think you'd say?

This very thing happened to a friend of mine, a film director named Tay Garnett.

And involuntarily, he shouted, *"God, keep me in the circle of Your love."*

Moments before, as he had buckled on his seat belt, he had whispered the same words. He always did—just by habit. He couldn't remember when he had started it, but it had become an almost unconscious part of getting in a car for him, as automatic as turning on the ignition key. Tay was a believer, though he didn't talk a lot about it; a film director talks about other things anyway, and not many people in the movie business seemed concerned with God.

So with Tay it was a private thing, this friendship with God.

He had his conversations with the Lord in quiet moments, and in little intimate ways he would indicate his sense of dependence on Him—like whispering as he buckled his seat belt, "God, keep me in the circle of Your love."

This afternoon he was directing a segment of a chase on a mountain road high above the Atlantic Ocean, and to demonstrate to the stunt driver and camera crew what he wanted to get, he chose to drive the car along the route he wanted it to take. He drove slowly and deliberately, purposely coming near the cliff edge to heighten the suspense of the sequence he was already filming in his mind, and just at the last second he cut the wheel to veer away from disaster looming before him—but the car didn't respond!

The wheels slid in the gravel, his speed actually increased, and while the crew watched in frozen horror, he plunged over . . . .

"God, keep me in the circle of Your love!"

About 400 feet below, a large tree, in full leaf, grew improbably from the sheer face of the cliffside. It was the only possible obstruction for hundreds of yards in any direction—and Tay's car dropped straight into it!

The impact demolished the car and broke Tay's back, but the rugged tree kept the VW from tearing through to the rocks waiting 300 feet further down. And while Tay, still fully conscious and strapped into the seat, waited and prayed, a rescue team was formed and lowered by ropes to the swaying tree. It took several hours of heart-stopping, courageous, commandolike effort, but the rescue team got Tay strapped onto a stretcher pack and raised by ropes and pulleys to the top. From there they rushed him to a hospital, where a waiting surgical team repaired the damage to his back.

In weeks, Tay Garnett was back at work, and he has directed a lot of film since then (I tell him he's spoiled thousands of feet of perfectly innocent film!). He's still a believer. And though he still doesn't collar people to share his faith, he's certainly not bashful about telling anybody who wants to know that there *is* a God in heaven—a God who waits to become involved in the immediate needs of human beings, when He's given half a chance.

And Tay knows it from experience!

As I think about his brush with death, my mind runs through the Bible again, looking again at the many, many last-minute rescues I've read about there. After Noah had preached to the people for 120 years while he was building the ark, the very flood that drowned every other living thing buoyed him and his family of eight to safety—just in the nick of time! (Genesis 6, 7, 8 and 1 Peter 3:20). God waited till Abraham was *100 years old* before He gave him Isaac, the son of promise—talk about waiting till the last minute! (Genesis 21). The children of Israel were *instructed to wait,* helpless, by the Red Sea until the army of the Egyptians was thundering upon them—and *then* the sea of deliverance opened (Exodus 14) and God was glorified in their rescue! If you want to read an exciting story of miraculous deliverance, get that chapter out and read it again.

King David had a lot of close calls, and the Psalms reverberate with his praise of the Deliverer. Have you ever read (through) the twenty-second chapter of 2 Samuel? It's a beautiful, powerful hymn to the One who had just saved David's life. And remember old King Hezekiah? Second Kings 20 records how he asked for, and *received,* an additional fifteen years of life after God had told him through Isaiah to get ready to die—another last-minute reprieve.

And one of the most touching scenes in all of human history was enacted on two wooden crosses on a first-century Judean hill.

As his life's blood oozed from his punctured hands and feet, dying for crimes he had committed, with absolutely no way left to help himself, a Jewish renegade turned his throbbing head to the tortured figure on the adjacent cross and said, "Jesus, Lord, remember me when thou comest into thy kingdom" (Luke 23:42).

Is that so different from "God, keep me in the circle of Your love"?

And from His own martyr's cross, suffering in sublime innocence, the Master of Life replied, "Verily I say unto thee, To day thou shalt be with me in paradise" (v. 43).

The Judge commuted his sentence, and the thief regained his life— forever.

This Jesus is the One who resisted the Devil's attempt to get Him to cast Himself down from a high place (Matthew 4:6), because David had prophesied *that the angels would catch Him* (*see* Psalms 91:11) and He's the One who heard Tay Garnett's cry from a falling car!

He's the One who still says to all believers, "Lo, I am with you always, even unto the end of the world" (*see* Matthew 28:20).

Matthew 4:1–7   Luke 23:39–43
2 Corinthians 1:8–11

17   MR. HUGHES GOT THE POINT

Most miracles seem so unscientific.

Folks who want to can often explain them away, in time, by calling them emotional experiences, or coincidences, or removal of psychosomatic symptoms, or countless other more inventive pooh-pooh's.

Well, here's one *nobody* can explain away.

This one's scientific!

Check it out with Howard Hughes, if you want to.

This one happened at one of the Hughes Aircraft installations, and the product of it is still in use there!

A friend of ours, Ray Anderson, works in a highly sensitive area of a Los Angeles space-related plant. Ray's a research technician whose hobby is flying his own homemade gyrocopter, so he's no far-out dreamer. He's a practical man who has to size up the reality of things and work with a precision unthinkable to most mortals. His highly disciplined work contributes to the fantastic success of America's space satellites.

Until two years ago, Ray, though not an atheist, had taken religion somewhat for granted, leaving his Episcopalian wife, Nancy, to get their kids to Sunday school without him. He couldn't see how spending time in some handsome old church on Sunday mornings changed anything very much, so he would take his gyrocopter to the desert most Sundays, and get "high" on reality!

He usually came back more charged up for the week than anybody else in the family, but if Nancy and the kids wanted to keep going to church, that was okay with him. He just didn't consider church attendance necessary.

Until—a couple of years ago. He began to hear about people who were having more than just humdrum religious trips. He heard accounts of supernatural happenings, of miracles—from friends. He *saw* people around him changing, heard his own wife telling him of impossible things occurring to folks who simply believed the Bible and called on the Name of Jesus!

This wasn't "church" or "religion," as he had known it—and it intrigued him. It called forth the researcher in him, and he began to investigate. He read *Nine O'Clock in the Morning* by Dennis Bennett, an Episcopalian priest! This man, a trained theologian, told of undeniable miracles, of supernatural encounters with a living God! He read my book *A New Song,* which talked about more miracles and a new dimension of life flowing from a mysterious-sounding experience called the "Baptism in the Holy Spirit."

He checked these things out in the *Manufacturer's Handbook*—the Bible—and decided he'd been missing out on a much higher reality than he could ever find in a gyrocopter *or* an Apollo rocket. Before too long, he met Jesus as Lord of his life and Baptizer in the Holy Spirit.

His life changed.

Oh, he was still involved in aerospace work, but he approached it with the fresh view of one who is being tutored by the One who spoke all things into existence. He was still a husband and father—but a better one. He was learning from a loving Father who wanted our personal relationships so much that He gave His only Son to rescue us from a fatal illness: sin.

Ray still had a wonderful brain, but now his intellect was bursting with new flashes of insight and understanding. And he wanted to share it all!

So he turned to one of the men closest to him, who worked in the inner sanctum at Hughes. They were together most of the time, in a dust and germ-free lab.

But the man was an atheist.

He didn't seem to grasp what Ray was trying to tell him, at all. No matter where Ray would begin, John seemed to tune him out after a short polite listen. It began to dawn on Ray that John was where *he'd* been just a short time before! Not that Ray had been an atheist, but maybe John's attitude was actually more honest, because he didn't pretend to believe in something that had no obvious effect on his daily life. He just flat didn't *believe*—so what could Ray say?

Nothing.

When the finality of this sank in, Ray was sitting at a bench doing some extreme precision work under a microscope. He was using a tiny machine-tooled punch *that John had designed and made* for the job at hand, installing delicate bearings in a critical point on a space satellite component.

While he worked, he thought. And his thoughts became sort of a prayer: "Lord, there's nothing else I can say to John. I'm going to have to leave him to You, because I just can't get through. His brain is in the way, and I understand that. It'll take a miracle, I guess . . . ."

His prayer was interrupted by a heart-stopping sight. The punch point had broken!

The tip of the punch was imbedded in a tiny bearing, and using the rest of the punch, he couldn't dislodge it. He tried continuing his work with the ragged punch, but only succeeded in ruining segments of the bearing retainer. It was hopeless; a new punch would have to be made, and this meant at least a day's delay.

Before he got up to tell John the sad news, Ray opened his drawer at the desk where he was working. He said later he couldn't remember why, unless he was planning to take out his Bible—but instead, he saw Dennis Bennett's book *The Holy Spirit and You* right on top. He casually opened it and saw that he'd turned to a chapter on miracles. This sentence, he remembers, caught his eye: *"God expects to do miracles, so Christians should never feel hesitant about asking for them."*

Well, Ray could sure use one now!

Still feeling a little sick about what had just happened, and hating to tell John, Ray picked up the punch again—and as he looked at it, *he was bathed in goose bumps!*

Where there had been an ugly jagged stump just a few moments before—there was now *the brightest, most perfectly machined point Ray had ever seen.* It took his breath away; it frightened him!

When he could bring himself to look at it closely under the microscope, he saw that the workmanship was exquisite—the Hughes shop could never duplicate it. And the *first* point was still there, imbedded in the bearing where it had broken off!

"John," Ray called out, "you've got to see this."

And John did see it. He saw the new point and marvelled at its obvious quality, he saw the old point sticking in the bearing, he saw the ruined retainer—and then he looked at Ray in bewilderment.

"Where did this new point come from?"

Ray told him.

There was silence for a while in that sterile lab. What can you say when you're confronted with a visible reality that can have no scientific explanation? John knew Ray hadn't left the lab, and the evidence was right there under the microscope. There could be no argument, no explaining this away.

"Ray," John said, "it had to happen the way you said—nothing else is *possible.*"

Then he continued: "I suppose if you believe that there's a God who can heal broken bones which are made of atoms and molecules, He can also heal broken metal which is also made of atoms and molecules. You know, if there were a Bible in modern English that I could understand, I might read it, but for some reason I just can't get much out of the King James Version."

Ray had a fast answer to that.

"It just happens," he said, almost laughing, "that my sister-in-law sent me a copy of a new, revised Bible in modern English which I received yesterday. It's right here in the desk drawer, and I'd be happy to lend it to you."

John took the Bible.

"I'll read it," he promised.

And as far as I know, he's still reading it!

I checked with Ray a couple of days ago, and he assures me that they're still using that punch with the miracle point out at the Hughes lab—and it's been over a year now! The man-made one lasted only a few minutes, but the new point seems better than ever after a year's use!

Yes, Mr. Hughes got the point. The physical one. But there's a much more valuable point involved—the spiritual one.

If you read the Genesis account of Creation, you'll see that God made all the physical things and set up the animal kingdom *before* He made man and placed him in charge. When the Lord God "breathed into his nostrils the breath of life; and man became a living soul" (2:7), He meant for this newly formed lump of clay to have dominion—rulership—over every other created thing on this planet! And over and over throughout the Bible, we read of the times when God changed the shape and the very physical makeup of people and objects to demonstrate His power—and to give us a flash example of the kind of existence He created *us* for!

Treat yourself to a few of these lightning flashes. Check Exodus 4:1-9 for the sight of the rod of Moses becoming instantly clean and water turning to blood. See a man *ordering the sun to stand still* for a whole day, in the name of the Lord (Joshua 10:12-14)—and the sun obeying! Skip back into Genesis 19:26 for a human being's turning to a salt statue—it really happened—and forward to 2 Kings 20:1-11 to watch God turn the shadow on a sundial *back* ten degrees!

I guess to have followed Jesus for a couple of days during His earthly walk would have turned any twentieth-century brain to Jello. Everywhere He went, He simply suspended the natural laws and the supposed scientific principles at will. He fed five thousand people from a handful of food, with twelve baskets left over; He changed water to rare old wine in an instant; He strolled on the surface of the Sea of Galilee as if it were Central Park; He called a man, dead and decomposing four days, back to healthy life. (Think of the chemical changes that had to take place in Lazarus's tissues and organs!) He passed through walls as if they weren't there!

No wonder modern man wants to do away with the miraculous—if he allows God to have *His* way, *anything* can happen!

It's very unsettling, isn't it?

As the brilliant ex-atheist, C. S. Lewis, in his *Miracles: A Preliminary Study,* says:

> You have had a shock like that before, in connection with smaller matters—when the line pulls at your hand, when something breathes beside you in the darkness. So here; the shock comes at the precise moment when the thrill of *life* is communicated to us along the clue we have been following. It is always shocking to meet life where we thought we were alone. "Look out!" we cry, "it's *alive!*"
>
> . . . There comes a moment when people who have been dabbling in religion ("man's search for God") suddenly draw back. Supposing we really found Him? We never meant it to come to *that!* Worse still, supposing He had found us?

He says it well, doesn't he?

Most people want a so-called safe religion—a "thinking man's approach." Well, they can have it—but chances are, God's not in it.

Two colleagues at Hughes found God in their laboratory—and He found them!

John 10:37, 38   John 11

18   MY VOCAL COACH, GIDEON

Ever read the story of Gideon and his fleece? If you haven't, check it out in Judges 6, 7, and 8. In fact, even if you *have* read it "once upon a time," a second go-round will do you a world of good. The fleece episode is in chapter 6.

The reason I bring it up is that I'd like to tell you my own fleece story.

It's pretty startling for the twentieth century but it really happened!

I had just put the finishing touches on the last two chapters of *A New Song,* my own spiritual autobiography. It was close to two in the morning and I was tired, but I heaved a giant sigh of relief as I sealed the much worked-over pages in a brown envelope for mailing. After breakfast I'd get them in the mail to Chicago.

Oh, yes—the mail.

I hadn't seen the mail that day, so as I passed through the kitchen on the way upstairs to bed, I stopped to sort through the stuff on the counter where it collects in piles—until Shirley lets out a wifely roar.

One return address caught my eye. The letter was from a long-time friend, a noted Bible scholar and teacher, so I opened it right away. My heart sank and the dark house seemed to grow even more still as I read,

Pat, I beg you *not to publish that book*. There's no way to calculate the harm it will do. Whole churches will split, thousands of earnest Christians will be plunged into uncertainty and confusion, and the cause of Christ will suffer greatly. I pray you'll reconsider and wait till you've had a lot more time to study and reevaluate your experiences.

The taste of the envelope glue was still on my tongue—and a gnawing foreboding was growing in the pit of my stomach.

I hadn't really wanted to write a book in the first place. The publisher, Bob Walker, and my dear friend, George Otis, had persuaded me that I had a story to tell, and that I *should* write it to encourage other people in every walk of life to seek the filling and guidance of the Holy Spirit. But I wasn't sure the great things that had happened at the Boone house were book material—or that many could be interested in our intensely personal experiences.

And I *knew* there were dangers!

There was a terrific danger to me, professionally. My agents had been reminding me that I was already considered a holy Joe, a Jesus freak, a weirdo to many Hollywood in-groups; and that publishing the account of miraculous doings at the Boone house might very well cast me forever in the role of Hollywood's answer to Oral Roberts!

And much more important, there was a very serious question as to how the Christian community would react to our incredible story. There would be mad controversy, I imagined, and lots of folks might feel I considered anybody who hadn't shared the depth of our experience as second-class Christians, or something. Plenty of confusion could resurface among believers in many principal churches over the work and power of the Holy Spirit today. I really didn't want to be a troublemaker.

But I *had* felt led, step-by-step, to tell our story—and I'd seen the spiritual transfusion it had been to many of our close friends and church brethren.

What was I to do? How could I know *God's* will in the situation?

As I turned out the kitchen light and slipped silently up the stairs to my bathroom, I remembered Gideon—*he* hadn't been sure of God's direction, so he laid out that fleece, beseeching the Lord to make His will unmistakable.

I decided to do that, too.

Kneeling by my bathroom window, looking out through shutters at the starlit sky, I whispered, "Oh Lord, I really want to do Your will. Have I been wrong to write this book? Should I have left out the controversial stuff about our experiences in Your Holy Spirit? Is it the wrong time to tell those things?

"Lord, I'll junk the whole thing. I'll tear up these chapters and cancel the book, if You want. Just please let me know.

"Father, I'm supposed to mail these last two chapters out tomorrow. Can I ask You to let me know—to show me Your will in some unmistakable way—*by noon tomorrow?*

"Thank You, my Lord."

And I dragged wearily into bed, just vaguely realizing I was asking an "impossible" thing, since I was only giving God less than ten hours to whip up some miraculous signpost for me!

Z-Z-Z-Z-Z-Z-Z—too late. I was gone.

Morning came quickly and I was up, dressed and ready for some backyard filming of a TV spot I'd agreed to do.

The cameraman arrived at 10 A.M., right on time, and started to set up—when they realized they'd *brought the wrong kind of film!* They were real pros, so this was embarrassing to them, and with much apologizing, they jumped into their van to run to get the right film.

As I let them out the front door, I was confronted by a Christian lady friend of ours and a man with her I didn't know, standing on our front porch. They had just arrived, hoping to see me for a few minutes.

Judy introduced her friend, a missionary named George Baker, and told me how he had a *prophetic word* for me—a message direct from the Lord!

I looked at him, back at her, saw they were both sane and composed and earnest and my heart began to pound as I remembered my request of the Lord just eight hours before!

"This is amazing!" I said. "I'm having to wait for a little while to do some filming out back. Let's go upstairs right now!"

For some reason my impulse was to go to our big bedroom where we pray so much and as we did, George explained that he was just back from an extended mission trip in India. He'd stopped over in Los Angeles, hadn't even seen his wife yet, but felt strongly impressed by God in prayer to come meet me and deliver some message which perhaps only I would understand!

Now, if this is foreign to you (it was new to me, then) you can read accounts of this operation of the Holy Spirit in both the Old and New Testaments:

Genesis 18:1–16   2 Samuel 12:1–12
Exodus 5:1–9   Acts 10
1 Samuel 9:15–17   Acts 21:8–14
            1 Samuel 15:1–23

I mean, I knew things like this had occurred to Abraham and Moses and King Saul and David and Peter and Paul—but in *Beverly Hills, California,* to Pat Boone?

(I *told* you this was pretty startling for the twentieth century!)

Well, we closed the bedroom door and began to pray. We just praised and thanked the Lord for a moment or two—and then George began to speak to me, his eyes closed, in a very authoritative way, the words flowing like a well-prepared, carefully thought-out message—much like someone reading an important telegram. I don't remember the words now, but the content of the message was that my submission to the Lord, and *our* yieldedness as a family, was pleasing to Him—and that He was going to "raise us up," meet our needs, and cause our testimony of His goodness to be heard *among the nations—that we were to share the rich provision of His love and His Spirit with others!*

The tears coursed down my face, my hands were raised, my lips stammered with praise. This man, George Baker, *knew nothing of my prayer* a few hours earlier! And yet, obeying a distinct nudge from the Lord during his own prayer time the night before, he stood before me now voicing God's specific answer to that prayer!

How wonderful!

Just then, while we were still praying and praising the Lord, the phone began to ring very insistently. I hoped someone would answer it elsewhere in the house—but on it rang. We had to pause—regretfully—and I picked up the phone with a touch of irritation in my voice.

"Pat . . . ? Is something wrong?"

It was Ann Hand, Shirley's best friend.

"No, Ann, we were praying, nothing's wrong. What's up?"

She said, "Oh, Pat, I just had to call you and Shirley to thank you for sharing your experiences with Lloyd and me. Since you've been telling us about *your* miracles, they're starting to happen to us! Lloyd's carrying his Bible with him when he travels and he comes home and shows me these neat things he's learned. We're even closer than before, and I can tell it's affecting our children in a lovely way. I don't know—I just felt I *had* to call you!"

Again—tears—goose bumps.

"Ann," I said, "this is . . . well, it's very interesting that you'd call about this right now. I've really been questioning whether I *should* tell other people about the miracles in our lives. Some of our religious friends have been begging me not to, for fear I'll just confuse folks and send them off on a lot of weird spiritual goose-chases. I'm really glad you called."

"Pat, you've *got* to tell other people about what God's done for you and Shirley! *Everybody* needs miracles today, especially in their families, and—oh, did you see this morning's paper? About the *miracle?*" she asked.

I told her I hadn't. What miracle?

"The girl who was blinded by the eclipse, when she looked at the sun, remember? Well, she can *see!* The doctor had said she was permanently blind—but the headline in the paper says she's had a miracle! I thought you'd want to read it."

I thanked Ann very enthusiastically, excused myself from George and Judy, and ran down to find the paper (which I wouldn't have seen that day if Ann hadn't called).

There it was, right on the second page.

"I Can See! I Can See!"

That was the headline, and the story went on to tell about Ann Turner's miracle, in Tipton, Indiana, suddenly receiving her sight after her eyes were hopelessly scarred—*through prayer*. Not just hers, but the believing prayers of three hundred groups and individuals over a two-month period. And the UPI story of May 8, 1970, quoted the doctor, David Thompson, an eye specialist, as saying definitely that Ann's blindness had been actual and physical, not hysterical, psychosomatic, or temporary. A miracle had happened!

The United Press and the L.A. *Times* were reporting miracles—

why couldn't I? Right then I knew *A New Song* would be published, with no apologies.

I looked at the clock on the kitchen wall.

It was almost noon.

My sweet Lord had accomplished what I had asked, in triplicate, and with minutes to spare—minutes in which to gather up some of the many lessons in that fantastic experience. I'm still gathering, too.

Jesus said, "Your Father knows what things you have need of, *before you ask Him*"! (*See* Matthew 6:8.)

I realized that while I was praying at 2:00 in the morning, the type had already been set for the *Times* story, the good things were happening to the Hands, and George Baker had already said, "Yes, Lord, I'll try to find Pat Boone and deliver Your word to him."

And I thought I was asking an impossible thing!

James 1:5–7   Deuteronomy 19:15 and 2 Corinthians 13:1
1 John 5:14, 15   Matthew 10:7, 8 and 10:24–42

19   MIRACLES HAPPEN EVEN IN NASHVILLE

Somehow, miracles of healing still seem the most dramatic to people, don't they?

Changed lives, healed marriages, saved souls, transformed characters, money miracles, dramatic encounters—all those things, as wonderful as they really are—fail to capture the wide-eyed attention of people as an undeniable physical healing does.

I guess that's because we're so involved with our own flesh. We're carnal, as Paul says. That seems to mean flesh-bound and flesh-motivated.

Jesus knew that, so physical healings sparked from His fingertips every day of His earthly ministry. Leprosy, blindness, blood disease, withered limbs, deafness and dumbness—every conceivable ailment known to man—He healed them all in bodies that were doomed to die anyway, so that "the works of God should be made manifest . . ." (John 9:3).

When John the Baptist was having some doubts about Jesus' being the Messiah, he sent his disciples to ask Jesus about it. Jesus said, "Go and shew John again those things which ye do hear and see: The blind receive their sight, and the lame walk, the lepers are cleansed, and deaf hear, the dead are raised up, and the poor have the gospel preached to them" (Matthew 11:4, 5).

The Lord cares about our bodies! He is willing, and able, to touch and heal them—especially when that manifestation of His power serves to draw souls to Him, through His Son Jesus. Besides, now that Jesus knows what it's like to be flesh-bound, having inhabited a body like yours and mine for thirty-three years, He's actually been known to *weep* for us, sharing our sorrow and suffering!

Paul says it: "For we have not an high priest which cannot be touched with *the feeling of our infirmities;* but was in all points tempted like as we are, yet without sin. Let us therefore come boldly unto the throne of grace, that we may obtain mercy, and *find grace to help in time of need"* (*see* Hebrews 4:15, 16).

My family and I are learning to approach that throne with more faith, and less fear.

One of the reasons is what happened to us in Nashville.

It's especially dramatic to us *because* it happened in Nashville! I grew up there, and love it, and hope to live there again soon. But I don't remember ever hearing about miracles happening in Nashville, even though there must be more Christian churches there in proportion to its population than any city in the world.

But folks in Nashville just don't believe in miracles. Especially church people. Oh, they believe in the miracles *in the Bible;* but we've all been taught for generations that God stopped all that miracle stuff in the first century, or at least by the time all the apostles died. All those

supernatural things were to "confirm the word" (*see* Mark 16:20)—
which is true—and once the Word was written and confirmed, God
went out of the miracle business. It doesn't *need* confirming anymore
(I wish that were true, but it isn't)!

And you know, if you don't believe in miracles, and expect them—
you're not apt to see many! Jesus Himself discovered that when He
went back to His own home town, "And He did not many mighty
works there *because of their unbelief*" (*see* Matthew 13:58).

Imagine our surprise recently, when Shirley and I were back home at
Mama's and Daddy's when some of our own church folks called late
in the evening and asked if they could bring over our dear friend Nancy,
who had enlarged nodes in her neck that were feared to be malignant.
They wanted us all to pray together for her healing! *They wanted to
ask God for a miracle!*

Friend, you would have to have grown up in Nashville to share our
excitement fully! This just isn't done! These were faithful, active
church folks; they'd been taught all their lives that miracles don't
happen. They know better. But now they needed a miracle, and their
own prayer and study of the Word, coupled with accounts of miracles
they'd heard about in our lives, made them want to "come boldly to the
throne of grace to obtain mercy" (Hebrews 4:16).

We urged them to hurry over, and when they arrived, we hugged
each other with a special first-century kind of warmth, interdependency,
and love. We were going to find out (together) if Jesus really is "the
same yesterday, to day and for ever" (Hebrews 13:8). It was exciting;
we were going to take the Lord at His Word, do all He commanded us
to do—and expect Him to do the rest, just like He did in the Bible.

I asked Nancy, our old school chum, to sit in a chair in the middle of
the room, so that we could all gather around her. She'd already had one
operation, the lumps had been removed and found malignant—and now
new ones had appeared! Surgery was scheduled, and the outlook was
pretty grim. She was happily married, the mother of two wonderful
children, and she wanted to live. She loved Jesus with all her heart,
and was willing to risk being "asked out of the synagogue" (*see* John
9:22–34) if He would touch her miraculously.

There were lumps in all our throats—love lumps—as we joined hands around her and prayed with a reverence and fervency that none of us had ever experienced before. I took a little jar of oil and anointed her forehead and her neck with little drops of it, obeying James's instruction, "Is any sick among you? let him call for the elders of the church [there were several in our little circle that night]; and let them pray over him, anointing him with oil in the name of the Lord: and the prayer of faith shall save the sick, and the Lord shall raise him up; and if he have committed sins, they shall be forgiven him" (James 5:14, 15).

And we prayed—oh, we *prayed!* With tears and supplication before the throne of God. We were people who had read about such things in Sunday school all our lives—but now we were *doing* it. And there came a moment when our prayer stopped; no one seemed able to utter a sound; there was an undeniable sense of His Presence in our midst. We knew He was answering our prayer.

There was silence, and then soft murmurs of thanksgiving. We all embraced again, and the meeting was over.

Except for one footnote.

Mama, who'd only recently been baptized in the Holy Spirit, had been praying softly in her prayer language, and just before our little circle broke up, a little phrase formed on her lips with a special urgency. As our friends were leaving, Mama told me the words to see if I might know their meaning: *"Talitha cumi."*

"Talitha cumi!" I ran out to the car, caught the folks just before they pulled away and assured them Nancy was going to be just fine. I could *promise* them!

Those words appear once, only once as far as I know, in the New Testament, and I guarantee you Mama didn't know them. Look them up in Mark 5:41!

Several weeks went by, and the nodes stopped enlarging. This was the *opposite* of what had happened before, and the doctor was at a loss to explain it. They should have been growing, not shrinking! He still advised the surgery, though he said that if he didn't *know* the lumps were there, he probably would not have noticed them.

Everybody kept praying, but with a sure sense that God was in control. Finally the day for surgery came, and Nancy's husband phoned us the great good news: The doctor had removed two tiny, harmless little growths—and they were not malignant! Nancy was well, and the doctor assured them there was absolutely no reason to fear a recurrence in the future.

A miracle had happened in Nashville!

Mark 16:15–18   Hebrews 5:6–9

20 MIRACLE OF A JEWISH MOTHER

I know Jesus loves Jewish mothers. He had one of His own!

This is one of the most delightful miracles that's happened to me, and I hope Judy doesn't mind my telling you about it.

Judy is the wife of a successful lawyer in Baltimore, and the proud young mother of four kids. They're a thoroughly Jewish family, and though they had not been devout religiously, their background and associations and heritage combined to make them proudly Hebrew.

So it was really "out of the blue" that a friend gave Judy a copy of *A New Song* a couple of years ago. It was only because she had been something of a Pat Boone fan during her teen years that Judy was even mildly interested in reading my story; but she did sit down one afternoon in Baltimore and began to read it.

She couldn't quit; it did "strange things" to her; it troubled her and brought up all kinds of questions—but she couldn't put it down. She told me later that the major effect the book had on her was to cause her to "just fall in love with Jesus!" She says she *knew,* by the time she finished reading, that Jesus was the Son of God, her Messiah, and she wanted to meet Him in the most urgent way. And she felt that she needed to get to me, to talk to me; but only so that I could point her surely to the One she now recognized as her Lord.

But her husband, Bernie, wanted to go to Las Vegas!

He had a vacation coming, and he'd decided he and Judy would go to Glitter City and see the Stars. It sounded like a perfect way to really unwind. It was the last thing in the world that Judy wanted to do now; she wanted to track me down somewhere—anywhere—and make contact with Jesus. But she was Bernie's wife, and agreed to "go where you go." So they made arrangements for their kids, hugged them good-bye, and boarded the plane for Vegas.

The first thing they saw when they landed was a billboard advertising PAT BOONE AT THE FREMONT! I was appearing in downtown Las Vegas —right then!

The next night they were in my dressing room backstage, she and Bernie. They had seen my late show, were very complimentary about it, and had asked the captain to bring them back to talk with me. Judy was so radiant and bubbly that I began to feel something was up.

I knew it was when she blurted out that she had just read my book, and that it had had a terrific impact on her. "Pat, I am just *in love* with Jesus! Is He really like you say?"

I laughed, glancing at Bernie (who seemed a trifle surprised), and assured her He *is* wonderful—that He is the Messiah, and that I was in love with Him, too. I told her I was experiencing miracles every day in my relationship with Him.

"Are you still baptizing people in your swimming pool?" she asked.

"I sure am, whenever anyone asks me to."

She hesitated just a second, and then continued, "What do you do here in Las Vegas, if someone wants to be baptized?"

"Well," I answered, "I've never been asked here, but I would sure find a way—why? Do you want to be baptized?"

"Yes," she shot back, "I do!"

I looked at Bernie. His mouth was open—he wasn't understanding this at all!

"Well, Judy," I said, "You're staying at Caesar's Palace, right? I'll do some checking in the morning, locate a baptistry in a local church— or a pool, if necessary—and come by and pick you two up tomorrow afternoon. Okay?

She assured me she'd be ready, and took her dazed hubby away. I praised the Lord when I saw we'd talked to 3 A.M.—*I* was bubbling, too!

I phoned the minister of the biggest Church of Christ in town the next morning, knowing they'd have a baptistry filled and ready, and asked if I could bring this lovely young Jewish girl over to be baptized. The minister had some mixed feelings about it, because my open testimony to the miraculous working of the Holy Spirit had caused some controversy in his congregation—but he could hardly let that prevent a young lady's obedience to the Lord in baptism. He told me the baptism water would be heated and ready.

So I picked Judy up at Caesar's and drove her to the church.

Bernie didn't come. He assured Judy that although he didn't really understand all of this, "If this is what you want, honey—if it'll make you happy—go ahead."

Judy was glowing. She said, "Pat, I don't know how to say this—but I feel like I'm about to be married!"

I got goose bumps—I knew the Lord had given her an insight that was straight from heaven. "Judy," I said, "you *are*. Most of my life, I've looked at baptism as a *command,* a necessary ritual or obedience. That's the way a lot of people are looking at a wedding ceremony now. They feel that if they love somebody, why get married? Just move in together, establish a relationship, and forget that old ritual of a ceremony. But most of those relationships don't last.

"Your relationship with Bernie began *before* you got married, didn't it? You loved him and committed yourself to him before you got to a wedding ceremony, didn't you?"

She nodded.

"But that ceremony made it *official;* it 'tied the knot'; in it, you and Bernie said to the world and to each other: This is for keeps. We're one. Call us *Mr. and Mrs.* from now on—forever!

"Well, Judy, you've just helped me to see baptism more clearly.

"This *is* your wedding ceremony—with Jesus! Jesus calls the church, the body of believers, His bride! You're already in love with Him, and He's so in love with you that He died for you, and has brought you tenderly to this moment. Your relationship with Him has already begun, but now you're about to say to the world, and to Jesus, and the very angels in heaven—from now on, we're *one!* We're committed to each other—forever!"

We were both in tears, and soon we stood in the water of the baptismal pool, with the young minister standing by. I asked Judy one question, the same question Philip asked the Ethiopian in chapter 8 of Acts, "Do you believe with all your heart, Judy?"

She looked up, her eyes brimming brightly, and said loud and clear, "I believe that Jesus Christ is the Son of God, and my Saviour and my Lord—and I love Him."

And I baptized Judy in the name of the Father, the Son, and the Holy Ghost. It was glorious!

Right after I raised her up from her watery "burial" before we left the pool, she asked, "Can I pray now?"

I assured her she could; and while the minister and I bowed, the tears running down my cheeks, Judy talked intimately to Him, her spiritual husband. It was beautiful, more lovely than I can describe. And why should I? It was strictly between her and Jesus.

On the way back to the hotel, the new "bride" asked me about the Baptism in the Holy Spirit, and if she was now entitled to receive it. Wow—she was *so* earnest, so anxious to "move on" with the Lord—to have everything He was willing to give her! I told her that of course she was; while she was so pure and clean and baby-new, right then was the perfect time to claim Jesus' promise from the Father in Luke 11:13 and Peter's Pentecostal promise in Acts 2:38. I had never before been in the situation of leading an individual into the Holy Spirit Baptism all by myself—but somehow I knew the Lord was not going to say *no*.

So, in my car in the parking lot of Caesar's Palace, Judy and I prayed for Jesus to baptize her with His Spirit—and He did!

It was still to be a few days before Judy had freedom of expression in her prayer language, but it came. And more importantly, such changes appeared in Judy! It became clear to everybody who knew her that she had been with Jesus, that she was somehow "a new creature" (*see* 2 Corinthians 5:17). There were powerful ripples through her close circle of family and friends, and many tests confronted her. But Bernie stood by her, her kids drew even closer, and before long her sister-in-law became a radiant Jesus person, too! Judy and Rhona are still making big waves in Baltimore, and the Son of God is making His Presence felt in and through them.

And just before I sat down to write this, Judy sent me the wonderful report that her dear Bernie has given *his* heart to the Messiah, too! Now they are truly *one,* in every important way there is—thank You, Jesus! Praise your lovely Name, Lord!

Jesus obviously cares deeply and personally for Judy. Is He remembering His days as a carpenter's son in little Nazareth, and His own precious Hebrew mother?

He first became flesh in a young Jewish girl, and she brought Him to the world.

And now He indwells another young Jewish girl, and she's brought Him to Baltimore.

Romans 6:3–11   1 Peter 3:18–22

21 BORN AGAIN AT EIGHTY

I'd like to share with you another miracle involving baptism.

Baptism itself is a miracle. You see that, don't you?

If it's not—it's nothing—just a ridiculous ritual, a "dunking" with less significance than bobbing for apples. But if it's what Jesus and Peter and Paul *say* it is—baptism is a supernatural happening, a cleansing of the spirit, a mystic wedding rite whose bridegroom is the very Son of God. It's a new-birth experience! A profound miracle with eternal consequences!

I used to think (because I'd been taught to) that the act of baptism was, itself, the new birth. And I still believe that there *is* a definite parallel between physical birth and water baptism; but now I understand that, as every human being was *conceived* and became existent as a creature before his natural birth experience, so each of us must be born again—conceived anew by the Spirit of God—deep within, in his own spirit level, before his *supernatural* birth experience in water baptism.

Otherwise, he'd be stillborn. The ritual of birth would have occurred, but there would be no life there. And that happens—a lot.

That must be why Jesus told Nicodemus, "Except a man be born of water and of the Spirit, he cannot enter into the kingdom of God" (John 3:5), and why Peter says that baptism is "the *answer* of a good conscience toward God" (*see* 1 Peter 3:21).

Nicodemus, in his amazement, knew Jesus was describing a *miracle!* He said, "How can these things be?" And Jesus said plainly that He was not talking about earthly, human, natural things—He was describing a supernatural, heavenly, miraculous operation. A lot of well-meaning church folks, like myself for many years, have made such a legalistic human thing out of baptism that it's lost its supernatural power in our lives; and that's not at all what Jesus wanted it to be.

In that same chapter of John is the most beloved verse in the Bible: "For God so loved the world, that he gave his only begotten Son, that whosoever believeth in him should not perish, but have everlasting life" (3:16). Jesus talks about believing in the Son of God as the cutting edge between life and death, as the *conception* that begets eternal life—and cheats Satan of another trophy.

But a lot of Christians go through life as embryos, only partly formed "new creatures," because they fail to move on to their water-birth experience! They don't have the power they're meant to have, they're not certain of their relationship to the Father, and they carry a nagging, convicting sense of guilt.

That's what brought eighty-year-old Mary to our house.

First, I received a letter in which she said she'd read *A New Song,* and had been deeply moved by my story, and wondered if I still baptized people in our swimming pool. She said she'd contacted the church I mentioned in my book (the one from which I was later "disfellowshiped") and asked to be baptized; but when she mentioned that it was because of reading my book that she *wanted* to be baptized, the person she was talking to seemed strangely cool toward her. So she wondered if I ever . . . ?

I called her immediately, and offered to bring the pool to *her,* if she couldn't come to my house!

The next day, the loveliest little white-haired, pink-cheeked, sunny eighty-year-old lady walked in our front door. With her were a couple of elderly lady friends who had driven her over. Shirley and I welcomed them with hugs, and ushered them into our den where we chatted a while. I wanted to know a little about Mary, and to read several Scriptures about baptism, to make sure she understood the beauty of this miracle that was about to happen to her.

Her clear blue eyes danced as she told me she'd been a Christian for fifty years, but had never been baptized—had rarely even thought about it, until she read *A New Song.* And somehow, reading about Bill Hayes and the young Jewish girl and others who had walked down into our pool, there arose in her a desire to experience this peculiar act, that she'd only heard passing references to in all of her fifty years as a church member. It was so moving to me that a woman of her age was willing to obey the Lord in such a curious, irrational, seemingly undignified way.

I asked, "Mary, isn't it wonderful to know you belong to Jesus?"

At that, her blue eyes seemed to cloud, and the smile left her face. "I don't know that," she answered quietly. "I guess that's why I'm here. In your book, you seemed so *sure* about Jesus and your relationship with Him—and I've never—really *known,* down deep, that I belong to Him. Yes, I guess that's why I'm here."

And I realized she had diagnosed her own predicament with the crystal-clear judgment old people often have. I opened my Bible, and asked her, "Mary, will you believe Jesus if He says it?"

"Of course, I will."

I turned to Mark 16:16 and read Jesus' own words, "He that believeth and is baptized shall be saved; but he that believeth not shall be damned."

I asked, "You believe, don't you, Mary?"

She answered, "Of course I do; I wouldn't be here if I didn't."

"And you're going to be baptized today—what else does Jesus say?"

She looked at where my finger was pointing, ". . . shall be saved."

"Do you believe Jesus, Mary?" I asked her. She assured me she did, and seemed as anxious to "get on with it" as I was!

Shirley led her out to the pool house where she changed into a muu-muu, and in just a few minutes, I was taking her by the hand and leading her down into the shallow end of our swimming pool. I asked her the one question I always ask, "Do you believe with all your heart, Mary, that Jesus is the Son of God?"

With a small, steady voice, she answered, "I believe Jesus is the Son of God."

I looked heavenward, raised my hand, and said, "Lord God, You hear those words. You say that if we confess You before men, as Mary has just done, You'll confess us in Heaven. We believe that Mary is precious to You, that she belongs to You now, and the angels rejoice with us because she obeys You today. And now, in obedience to the example and command of our Lord Jesus, I baptize you, Mary—in the Name of the Father, and of the Son, and of the Holy Ghost." And I buried her in the water—and raised her to newness of life! With the water streaming through that snow-white hair, we hugged and thanked the Lord together. If there was anybody around that pool who wasn't shedding tears of joy, I didn't see them.

In just a few minutes more, Mary was changed and dry and ready to go. As her two friends passed before her through the front door, Mary stopped and turned around. She looked at Shirley, her eyes open wide with wonder; she paused just a second, and said slowly, "You're right —I know—*I know!*"

Her eyes brimmed full, she squeezed Shirley's hand and added, "I'll remember this day as long as I live."

Which was one week.

We received word that dear, blue-eyed, pink-cheeked Mary lived one week after she was baptized. And so she had one week of *knowing* in eighty years; and if it had to be just one—I'm glad it was that last one.

Do you think it was an accident—a freak coincidence—that brought Mary to our house so near to the end of her earthly days? I don't. I believe with all my soul that this Jesus, to whom she'd pledged her allegiance fifty years before, had led her to this moment of obedience, so she could come to Him, *knowing* she was His.

And what made the difference?

A miracle called baptism.

Now I see Peter's invitation on the day of Pentecost so much more clearly. He said, when the huge crowd, which had begun to see the miracle power of God manifested all around them, asked how they should respond to this, "Repent [turn toward God, experience the *conception* of new life within—that takes care of your future] and be baptized . . . in the name of Jesus for the remission of your sins [experience the new water birth, like a baby does—that takes care of your past, with its sin-stains], and ye shall receive the gift of the Holy Ghost [that's for the power to live *now*—like a true child of God] (Acts 2:38).

Jesus had said He'd give Peter the "keys to the kingdom" (Matthew 16:19)—and he used them that day! What a tragedy that so few of us, even dedicated disciples of Jesus, ever use all three keys. We either stay embryos, never experiencing a water birth with its cleansing power; or we stay little children spiritually, never asking for and receiving our inheritance—that mighty filling with the Holy Spirit and the spiritual gifts that will give us the muscle and weapons to be "sons [and daughters] of God" (John 1:12).

Nothing I know of in the Christian life happens automatically.

You *ask* for salvation. You *ask* to be baptized. And you must *ask* for the gift of the Holy Ghost (*see* Luke 11:13). You *ask* for forgiveness (*see* 1 John 1:8, 9). And you *ask* for the gifts of the Spirit (*see* 1 Corinthians 12:31 and 14:1). All these things have your name on them, like presents under the tree—but God, our Father, and the Giver of all good and perfect gifts, wants us to come to Him and raise our hands—and *ask*.

Miracles seem to happen to children—even when they're eighty years old.

---

1 Peter 3:18–22   Hebrews 5:12 through 6:1–6
John 1:29–34

22   A STREET-CORNER MIRACLE

This happened just today, so I'll tell it while it's hot!

I took some time off from the typewriter to do some jogging, hoping to keep my body in shape while I'm spending an inordinate amount of time staring at this gray hunk of metal and poking through my brain, looking for the words to tell you about these "touches of God" in our lives.

Even when you're burning to tell something—as I am—it's still a tough job to get it on paper in just the way you want to say it. So I took a break; it was a spur-of-the-moment decision, and I tossed on my jogging jacket, a baseball cap, and headed down Sunset Boulevard.

I'd chugged along for about a mile, running with the traffic along Sunset so that I wouldn't likely be recognized and stopped by tourists (they'd only see my back till they were already past me), when a Cadillac slowed ahead, pulled to the curb and waited. I huffed and puffed on by, and as I did, I saw the driver straining to get a good look at me. I just smiled and kept going, rounding the corner ahead and jogging up a side street.

The Cadillac followed, passed me again, pulled to the curb and waited. This time, as I approached, the driver leaned over and rolled down the window toward me and asked me for a moment of my time. I slowed to a stop and bent down to look in. The man, obviously a well-to-do businessman, introduced himself and said, "Forgive me for stopping you, Pat, but I felt I just had to. I've just finished reading your book *A New Song* and have felt envious of your relationship with the Lord. I've been praying and asking the Lord if it would be possible to meet you somehow—and as I was headed home just now, there you were, running along right out on Sunset! I really hesitated to bother you, and yet . . . ."

I didn't let him finish. I laughed and shook his hand and assured him that I recognized God's calling card. It was obvious to me that this meeting hadn't just happened. The timing was too perfect; he'd just been asking our mutual Lord for a minor miracle, and was driving along Sunset headed home; I'd taken a break from writing about miracles wrought by this same Lord, and decided spontaneously to run down that same stretch of boulevard—at that exact time! Two minutes earlier or later, and the meeting would not have occurred.

Who do you think can arrange things like that?

So we exchanged phone numbers, I invited him to worship with us at Church on the Way in Van Nuys, and also invited him to come to the once-a-month Bible studies in our home. He apologized for "having the shakes" all of a sudden, and I chuckled, explaining that he was having a very normal human reaction to the realization that the God of heaven and earth had *heard him*—and is personally taking a hand in his life. As we parted, I added, "Don't worry; the Lord will take it from here!"

And I know He will—thank You, Jesus. I love You.

> Oh, that men would praise the Lord for his goodness, and for his wonderful works to the children of men! For he satisfieth the longing soul, and filleth the hungry soul with *goodness*.

> *See* Psalms 107:8, 9

In Jesus' first sermon, recorded in Matthew 6, He talked about praying secretly, so that our Father could reward us *openly*. And He added, ". . . for your Father knoweth what things ye have need of, before ye ask him" (v. 8).

Does it seem just too far-out to think that this street-corner meeting was actually arranged by God? Well, take it up with Moses; his so-called chance meeting took place in the bullrushes (Exodus 2). And the Ethiopian treasurer; his so-called coincidence occurred on the dusty road to Gaza (Acts 8).

And take it up with Zaccheus; he was in a tree when Jesus happened along (Luke 19). In fact, just take it up with Jesus.

He spent a lot of time on street corners.

23   THE LAMB AND THE LION (MY SON, THE JUNKIE)

This is the story of a modern Jew who discovered that the Lion of Judah is also the Lamb of God.

That man is Irv Kessler, and he's my partner in a small, growing Jesus-music record company which we now call LAMB AND LION. We call it that because I'm a Christian and he's a Jew—and we have the same Rabbi.

His name is Jesus.

But before Irv ever knew this Lamb of God, he became a very successful executive with a major international record company. He knew practically everything about the production and distribution of records, the warehousing and accounting pitfalls, the manufacturing and packaging and costs and profits—and he made a lot of money at it!

He had a wife and family, two sons and a daughter, and he loved them. He was awfully busy, but he provided a good home for them and gave them whatever they needed. They had no time for religion, or any need for it, as far as Irv could see. They were "doing fine."

Until teen-aged David became a drug addict.

I'd like my brother Irv to tell his own story.

God gave us a miracle! Because of this miracle, I am now a Hebrew-Christian—a completed Jew. It all came about through my son David's being involved in a series of tragedies resulting from his very serious drug addiction problem.

David was on drugs from the age of fifteen through eighteen. He was surely dying before our very eyes and there was nothing humanly possible that we could do to stop it. He had taken all kinds of drugs over these three years, including marijuana, Methedrine, Seconal, LSD, and finally heroin. He was taking as many as thirty Seconals a day, enough to kill anyone, but had built up a resistance to this drug. We had taken David to doctors, psychiatrists, psychologists, and group therapy but nothing seemed to work with him. My son led a clean life and had been an all-star baseball player in the Little League. He was just like any other kid that belongs to a normal American family, but now he was heading for the grave because of his drug addiction.

David was arrested many times as a juvenile for being under the influence of narcotics and had spent time in juvenile hall. The culmination of these arrests came on the first Friday night in October, 1969. He was home in our kitchen with about thirty dollars worth of heroin in his possession. My twenty-year-old daughter was also home. I was visiting someone in Burbank where my little boy was spending the weekend with friends. My wife, a registered nurse specializing in cardiac care, was working that night at the hospital. The drug problem in our family caused this wonderful woman to attempt suicide twice. Once she tried to run her car off a cliff, but failed; the second time I wrestled a butcher knife away from her in our kitchen.

Because David was without his hypodermic needle and under the influence of Seconal at the time, he took an eyedropper, broke off the end, and started to file it down to a point. He was going to try to inject that heroin into his vein with this eyedropper. Had he been successful one of two things would have happened—he would have either overdosed or bled to death.

Seeing what David was trying to do, my daughter called my wife at work. My wife immediately called the police, giving them permission to break into our house and arrest David. The very moment she was calling the police I was in Burbank visiting a lady whose brother-in-law had been helped by a narcotic rehabilitation organization called Teen Challenge, of which I knew nothing. Previously we had tried everything to help him, and were now at the end of the road. Upon hearing about Teen Challenge I thought perhaps this might be the last chance to help him, and at that moment I called my wife at the hospital. As I spoke to her about Teen Challenge, she interrupted to tell me the news about what had happened with David at the house and that she had called the police. I raced out the Ventura Freeway to my house to try and save my son from the police, not even knowing what I would have done had I reached him before they did. It is a natural instinct for parents to protect their children.

When I arrived at my house, there were four police cars parked in front and about fifty people on the lawn. Not until I started walking up the driveway did I realize I didn't know whether my son was dead or alive in that house. When I walked into the kitchen there he was on a kitchen chair with his hands handcuffed behind him. Four officers stood around him while four more officers combed the house for additional drugs.

Peering up at me from under all of his long hair and under the influence of narcotics, David looked like a terrified animal. He was thin, emaciated, and even looked as if he had a touch of hepatitis. He was crying and when he saw me he pleaded, "Dad, please help me!" I must admit that in that moment I felt more helpless than at any time in my life. I did not know what to do for my son. A coward, worried about what my friends and associates would think of me if they found out that I had a son on drugs, I ran away from the problem instead of trying to solve it. I had allowed my wonderful wife to bear the brunt of this ugly situation because I had given up all hope of ever helping my son. I loved my boy—make no mistake about it—but I was also very self-centered and concerned about my image. Outwardly I hated my son for what he was doing to me and my family, but down deep in my heart I was breaking up into a million pieces because I loved him so very dearly. My wife never gave up—she always said that as long as she had a breath in her body she would try to find a way to save our son.

That night they took David to the West Valley police station and then moved him to the Van Nuys jail for transfer to county jail on Monday morning. Because he had turned eighteen in August, 1969, two months earlier, he was now booked as an adult. We let him stay in the Van Nuys jail Friday night, Saturday night and Sunday.

Sunday night something possessed me to telephone the sister of the woman in Burbank who had told me about Teen Challenge. My wife and I talked to her sister, Sharon, for about an hour. She told us about how her husband had been helped at Teen Challenge and we told her what had recently happened to David, although she already knew about some of his problems through my communication with her sister. When Sharon heard that our son was going to the county jail on Monday, she proceeded to tell us about the many times her husband had been in and out of that same jail for burglary, robbery, and narcotic offenses. At the close of our telephone conversation we knew one thing—that no matter what David had done, county jail was not the solution to his problem.

Sharon said that if we could get him out of jail and take him to the Cucamonga Teen Challenge Center (she had already talked to Cliff Morrison, the director), they would interview him on Monday. This was our last hope so we made the decision to bail him out.

That Monday I shall never forget at Teen Challenge in Cucamonga. Walking into the reception house I thought that the boys must have just come out of chapel for they all had Bibles in their hands. Their hair was cut short and neat and they were clean-shaven. They just radiated with warmth and friendship. Seeing that we were strangers they shook my hand saying, "Praise the Lord; praise the Lord!"

I had never heard that expression before and did not know what they were talking about. However, following that old adage, "When in Rome, do as the Romans," I answered, "Yes sir, praise the Lord, brother."

They interviewed my wife and myself for about forty-five minutes. Manny Ganzales, a former addict for about eighteen years, told us, "If David sincerely wants help down deep in his heart, we will take him. But I now must talk to him to find out." These counselors, having been addicts themselves, cannot easily be fooled; they can spot a phony a mile away if he is trying to play games with them.

My wife and I went out on the porch while Manny and David talked. Never had I heard such loud singing and hand-clapping as was coming from the house across the street, which I later learned was serving as their chapel. This was my first exposure to such things, and I remarked to my wife, "Marion, I believe we are involved with holy rollers."

David came out in about an hour with Manny, who said, "I think David really wants help. We will take him." At that time there were only two beds available at Cucamonga Teen Challenge because this is such a very busy place. There was a boy coming in from Bakersfield, California, to fill one bed. I now know that God had saved the remaining bed for my son. We had packed a bag for him and put it in the trunk of our car in the hope that something would happen that day. I tell you in all sincerity that if we had had to take him away from the center that Monday morning I do not know where we would have gone with him. All the money in the world would not have saved my son's life. We would have taken him back home to certain death; but the Lord had other plans for David.

He came to trial one month later in the Van Nuys courtroom. It was planned that I would pick him up about a quarter to six on the appointed morning. At the beginning of the fourth week, having had no conversation with him for three weeks, I called him up.

"Dad, I have a surprise for you," he said.

I had not heard him use that word "surprise" in at least three years. "Dave, if it is good news please tell me now because your mother and I certainly could use it."

"No, when you get out here I will tell you about it." For that week we were on pins and needles. When I got out there at six o'clock on the morning of the trial they brought him down into the kitchen. He *did* have a surprise. First of all, he had a haircut. Also, he had put on at least ten to fifteen pounds. I hardly recognized him. At that point, the trial ceased to worry me even though David had three felony charges against him. I was so overjoyed at his physical appearance.

Once in the court I stopped our attorney in the lobby. "Loren," I said, "something revolutionary has happened to David in thirty days." With that, I gave him some of the Teen Challenge literature. "I am going to have to point him out to you," I said.

When he saw David in the courtroom, he said, "I simply can't believe it!"

Upon my insistence that it really was David, the lawyer shook hands with him and said, "When this case is called I will ask the judge for a conference in chambers and, in view of the present circumstances, request clemency."

Two hours later, after the case was called, he came out of chambers saying, "Everything is fine; there will be no trial." I will never forget that moment. On the way home David asked, "Dad, would you mind stopping at that store across the street?" I took a look to where he pointed, then took a second look. "What are you going to do over there?" I asked, for the sign read VALLEY BOOK AND BIBLE STORE.

"I want to buy a Bible." I almost ran the car into the concrete island in my haste to turn around and go back. While David talked to the saleslady, my wife and I walked to the front of the store and cried like babies. It was then that we realized something wonderful had come into his life.

In the middle of December, 1969, a month later, I witnessed the water baptism of my son in the First Assembly of God Church in Pomona, California. One would think that I, a Jew and non-Christian, would be vitally opposed to something like this. Instead, it was the proudest moment of my life! I knew that my boy had found something that I did not have, and I was actually a little jealous.

A week and a half afterward, following one of the Teen Challenge functions, David asked me, as he had so many times before, "Dad, have you accepted Christ as your Saviour yet? Do you know the Lord?"

It was near Christmas. When I looked at him in that lobby it was just as if there were two spotlights coming out of his eyes. They shone like diamonds. I threw my arms around my son and kissed him, saying, "Yes, Dave, I have found Him." So it was, that in December of 1969 I accepted Jesus Christ as my Lord and Personal Saviour. This experience paved the way for the happiest New Year I have ever known. I was now a Hebrew-Christian.

The next Father's Day, June 21, 1970, David and my family gave me what is now one of my prize possessions—a Bible. On the flyleaf he had written the Scripture, Luke 15:20, "And he arose, and came to his father. But when he was a great way off, his father saw him, and had compassion, and ran, and fell on his neck, and kissed him." How beautifully that parable describes how I feel about my son and the graciousness of God in David's life and mine!

In the fall of the same year the Lord called my precious wife to be with Him. He had graciously allowed her to witness the healing of her son, and the conversion of her husband. In her going, God was able to bring a powerful testimony of His ability to redeem to all our Jewish relatives and friends. The Teen Challenge young people from all of Southern California shared with us in her last services. Surely our God is a very present help in time of need.

(Reprinted from VOICE)

I don't know how Irv's story affects you—but I've had to dry my eyes and blow my nose before I can add a postscript. Maybe it's because I know Irv and Dave so well, and am exposed to the glow of their warm radiant faith often. I know who they are today—and where they've come from.

This is a miracle of major proportions.

And, as frosting on the cake, I want you to see two documents—one a certificate recognizing Dave's outstanding scholastic record at Pierce College last year, and the rehabilitation of a drug-wrecked mind; and the other a citation of honor from the U.S. Department of Defense and General Creighton Abrams, then commander of our forces in Viet Nam! This second document came about when young David Kessler spent five months in army camps all over South Viet Nam, traveling with other ex-drug addicts from Teen Challenge, ministering to thousands of our GI's who had become junkies while in service for Uncle Sam!

The officers and doctors in Viet Nam acknowledged that the Teen

LOS ANGELES PIERCE COLLEGE

ALPHA GAMMA SIGMA
scholastic honor society

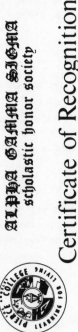

Certificate of Recognition

awarded to ___DAVID ALAN KESSLER___

for Outstanding Scholarship & Placement on the
Dean's List at Los Angeles Pierce College

given this ___twentieth___ day of ___November, 1973___

Edward Sister
College President

Daniel Chudnofsky
President, Associated Student Body

Wm. Benjamin H.
Dean of Instruction

Frank Osterman
President, Alpha Gamma Sigma

Department of Defense

United States Military Assistance Command, Vietnam

Certificate of Appreciation

is awarded to

Mr. DAVID A. KESSLER

FOR YOUR OUTSTANDING CONTRIBUTION TO THE JOINT EFFORT DIRECTED AT THE PREVENTION OF DRUG ABUSE IN VIETNAM DURING THE PERIOD 18 OCTOBER 1971 TO 24 FEBRUARY 1972. YOUR PERSONAL SACRIFICE IN PRESENTING YOURSELF DIRECTLY TO THE TROOPS AND THE SINCERITY WHICH IS MANIFEST IN YOUR UNSELFISH AND COMPLETELY VOLUNTARY VISIT TO THIS WAR ZONE, MERITS THE GRATITUDE OF EVERY SOLDIER AND CITIZEN. YOUR OWN KNOWLEDGE OF AN EXPERIENCE WITH THE DRUG CHALLENGE, COUPLED WITH YOUR WILLINGNESS TO SHARE THAT KNOWLEDGE AND EXPERIENCE, HAS PROVIDED A MUCH NEEDED CHANNEL OF COMMUNICATION AND RAPPORT TO POTENTIAL AND COMMITTED DRUG USERS. THIS COMMAND RECOGNIZES AND IS GRATEFUL FOR THE IMPRESSIVE CONTRIBUTION YOU HAVE MADE, BOTH TO INCREASE THE OVERALL EFFECTIVENESS AND MORALE OF UNITED STATES FORCES IN VIETNAM AND TO PROVIDE INVALUABLE INDIVIDUAL GUIDANCE AND ASSISTANCE TO THOUSANDS OF AMERICA'S SERVICEMEN.

SAIGON, VIETNAM

Date 18 February 1972

CREIGHTON W. ABRAMS
General, United States Army

MACV 1776 (6-68)

Challenge program, a total spiritual approach, was the *only real effective* "rescue operation" the government had found! Thousands of our GI's discovered, while in far-off Indochina, that Jesus is still the Great Physician.

And young Dave Kessler, son of a Jewish record executive, who scarcely a year before had cried to his anguished father, "Dad, please help me!"—from the very brink of hell—was one of that little volunteer band who brought Doctor Jesus to them.

The Lion of Judah has not lost His power, nor the Lamb of God His compassion.

And He continues to do the most surprising things! Remember, He's the one who chose the Jewish businessman, Matthew (Levi) to be one of His original twelve disciples—and to write the first book of the New Testament! Perhaps He knew that Matthew could be counted on to keep the record straight.

As Matthew tells the story of his own enlistment (Matthew 9:9) he goes on in the next few verses to show that Jesus led him first *back to his own house,* sat down and ate with him and his business friends, and was severely criticized by the religious leaders of His day for associating with "tax collectors and sinners."

It was *there* that Jesus said—perhaps in the kitchen of this businessman's home—"They that are well need not a physician, but *they that are sick."* (*See* Matthew 9:12.)

Two messianic believers: Irv Kessler and Matthew. Two Jewish businessmen, following the Lion of Judah, the Lamb of God. And one David, the son, giving his very life to the Son of David.

Matthew 10:5–8   Matthew 21:28–32
Luke 15:3–7

24 THROUGH PRISON DOORS

A man called my office and asked me to pray for a woman named Rhoda who was dying of cancer. She was not related to him, but he felt an unusual compassion for her; and he said he also felt that the Lord would touch her if I would go to the hospital in Santa Monica and pray for her.

I appreciated the man's concern, but honestly, I wasn't eager to get involved. The woman was floating in and out of a coma; her brain was completely permeated by the tumor that had overwhelmed it, and there was no hope. On top of that, she wasn't even a believer in Jesus—or at least, she'd never given any public evidence of it. Her background was Jewish, but she'd drifted into some "mind-science" religion hoping to find answers. Obviously, she hadn't found what she needed.

Still, I found it hard to say no. Something pulled me toward her.

I think it was more my concern for the man who called than for the woman. Raised a Catholic, he'd just recently made a real commitment of his life to Jesus. He was really turned on. Suddenly, Jesus wasn't a plaster figure permanently hanging, distorted and pathetic, from a cross on the wall—He was the living Son of God, powerful and present—and still in the miracle business! His faith was strong and optimistic, and I didn't want to do anything to dampen it.

So, one afternoon, in the midst of a normally hectic day, I turned down Wilshire Boulevard, and headed west toward the beach—and Santa Monica.

I found the little hospital, asked for the woman's room, and soon stood at her bedside. I saw a wasted little Jewish lady (in her middle fifties, I think) staring at the ceiling, apparently seeing nothing. I spoke to her but saw no response, no indication that she heard me at all. I tried again, with no reaction, and began to feel pretty foolish. My own discomfort was compounded by the fact that there was someone in the other bed, another lady, and she was evidently wondering what my point was. She explained that the woman I'd come to see rarely gave any indication that she knew what was going on around her, and hadn't made any sounds for days.

She recognized me, and asked if I was related to the poor lady; I told her I wasn't, but had simply come to visit her and pray for her, at the request of a mutual friend. Well, this woman thought that was "fine," and volunteered that she was a member of some religious-science group. At that point, a couple of her friends came to visit her, and I felt more in the spotlight than ever. I just wanted to leave, as quickly as possible.

So I took the little Jewish woman's thin hand, and with my back to the others in the room, sort of whispered to her that I'd come to pray for her in Jesus' Name, and that I hoped she could hear me and would pray with me. And I did pray. I really didn't have faith to ask much of the Lord (to ask Him to heal her on the spot or anything), but I asked Him to have His perfect will with both of us, to use our joined hands as a point of contact, an agreement for His purpose in her life.

When I finished my rather desperate prayer, I opened my eyes—and she was looking at me! There had been no movement, no evidence that I was getting through, but now her eyes were trained on me, and there seemed to be a questioning in them—a wonder.

I didn't know what to do then. I tried to talk to her, but she couldn't answer. She really seemed to be trying to communicate with me, just through her eyes, but it seemed hopeless. After a few frustrating moments, she appeared to give up the effort and her eyes returned to their vacant gaze at the ceiling.

I breathed another prayer, gently squeezed her hand, and left.

What else could I do?

I've rarely felt so defeated, so ineffectual, as I did on my drive home that afternoon. Had I done the right thing? Should I just have "left well enough alone"? Was my faith too small to meet the need of this dying woman? Had I failed to be bold enough, or sensitive enough to the Spirit? One thing for sure: I was no Peter or James or John.

Peter or James or John—something was nudging me, tugging at my spirit. What was it? That evening, as I told Shirley about what had happened, or *hadn't* happened, I confessed that I felt I'd missed something somewhere; I felt that the circumstances of the situation added up to an opportunity to see God working miraculously—and somehow, I was letting Rhoda down.

Rhoda.

Wait a minute—wasn't that name in the Bible somewhere?

There was a quick little leap inside me, down deep. I seemed to remember that name from the Book of Acts somewhere! If I could find it, maybe there would be a clue to the miracle in this situation.

In minutes, I'd found Rhoda in chapter 12 of Acts. The Apostle Peter had just been miraculously released from prison by an angel, and stood knocking at the door of Mary's house, where many disciples were praying. His knocking interrupted their praying, and *a Jewish girl named Rhoda* came to see who it was! She was so stunned to see Peter standing there (they had been praying for him in prison) that she left him waiting outside the locked door while she ran to tell the others. An almost comical moment followed in which the disciples debated about who it could be, an apparition, an angel, or Rhoda's imagination, while Peter continued to knock at the locked door. Eventually, somebody suggested that they open the door to settle the controversy, and they did— and Peter walked in!

I rejoiced.

I felt the Lord had just shown me what to do. I was in Peter's shoes, knocking at a locked door, and a Jewish lady named Rhoda was on the other side of that locked door, looking at me, unable to open the latch and let me in, or even to communicate with me, except through her eyes!

Other Scriptures were tumbling into my consciousness now: Luke 24 and John 20, where Jesus miraculously appeared in the midst of the disciples *"when the doors were shut."* He is not bound by our walls! In 1 Peter 3:18 and 19, Jesus, "being put to death in the flesh but [made alive] by the Spirit . . . *preached unto the spirits in prison."* Again— He could not be kept out! Then there was His own declaration in Luke 4:18, "The Spirit of the Lord is upon me, because He hath anointed me to preach the gospel to the poor; he hath sent me to heal the brokenhearted, *to preach deliverance to the captives* . . . ." (Italics are mine.)

I knew that if an angel could penetrate Peter's prison and set him free, Jesus could surely reach Rhoda. No cancerous paralysis, no human incapacity could prevent the entrance of the Son of God, *if* He were invited in. My job was to encourage her to invite Jesus into her prison.

I could hardly wait to get back to the hospital the next day.

Amazingly, Rhoda's roommate was alone and asleep, and Rhoda herself lay motionless, just as I'd left her before—imprisoned and helpless— but awake.

I took her hand, and again her eyes turned toward me, though not another muscle moved. I began to tell her of what the Lord had shown me, that her name was in the Bible, and I read her the account in Acts 12. I read her the other Scriptures, told her about the thief on the cross who had been dying with no hope and described how Jesus took him to paradise with Him upon a simple confession and reception of His Lordship, and finished by reading Jesus' own words (italics are mine) in Revelation 3:20:

Behold, I stand at the door, and knock: if any man hear my voice, and open the door, I will come in to him, and will sup with him, and he with me.

"Rhoda," I whispered, looking into her wondering eyes, "Jesus is knocking at the door of your heart. You can't open the physical door, and neither can I. But right now, in the prison of your own body, if you'll just say, 'Yes, Jesus,' in your heart, I know He'll come in and free you forever. Satan thinks he's got you locked away for eternity, but you can let the Son of God in right now, and all the devils in hell can't stop you! Do you believe me? Do you believe that Jesus *is* the Son of God and your Messiah—and will you open your heart and let Him in? Just say, 'Yes, Jesus,' in your mind and heart, Rhoda; just say, 'Yes, Jesus . . .'."

And tears trickled from those motionless eyes, running across dying cheeks to the pillow.

I know she heard and understood. **I believe** she said, "Yes, Jesus," though I couldn't hear it. I believe Jesus entered her prison and set her free.

I'm looking forward to meeting Rhoda in heaven. Her body perished a short time later, but I believe with all my heart that the Jesus who brought me to her bedside has taken her to paradise with Him—because she opened the door.

Psalms 142

25 THE MIRACLE OF HEALTH

For fifteen years, I had a virus attack twice a year.

I'm a very healthy guy, but *everybody* comes down with the flu now and then, right?

Wrong.

I don't anymore; I've had the bug—just briefly—*one time* in the last five years! Why I even had it that once, I'm still trying to figure out.

But it's true that for the previous fifteen years, almost like clockwork, I came down with a roaring flu each winter and spring. You know what I'm talking about—the headache, the sore throat, then the fever, the stomach turning inside out—the works. And it always hit me the worst right where I live—in my throat!

That meant knocking my voice out of commission for several weeks, because usually I would strain it while I was coming down with the bug; then the infection would last a week or so; and then it would take a couple of weeks for my vocal cords to regain their strength. I eventually came to know all the antibiotics by their first names!

But soon after my "mountaintop experience," in which I turned my life over to Jesus and asked Him to be my Lord as well as my Saviour, the Holy Spirit began to illuminate passages of Scripture to me that I'd been skimming over all my life.

One of those passages was Mark 16:18. "They shall take up serpents; and if they drink any deadly thing, it shall not hurt them; they shall lay hands on the sick, and they shall recover."

I was already keenly aware of the preceding three verses, in which Jesus commands us to believe and be baptized, and that "signs shall follow them that believe." He refers specifically to casting out demons and speaking in tongues. I had learned that Jesus was speaking to *everyone who believes,* and so had already claimed my prayer language, and knew what it was to speak in tongues, praising my Saviour with my spirit as well as my mind.

(I hadn't encountered demons yet, or had occasion to exercise Jesus' authority in that area—but it was to come.)

It wasn't until the fall of 1969, as I was approaching the flu season, that Mark 16:18 lit up before my eyes. *I suddenly saw the unavoidable virus as a serpent,* attaching itself to me like the viper who sprang at the Apostle Paul in Acts 28! It happened on the island of Melita, and the "barbarians," the local folks who saw this terrible thing happen, drew back and waited for Paul's arm to swell up and for him to keel over dead. They *knew* the deadly power of that poisonous viper! It must have been tremendous.

But all they saw was Paul shaking the "beast" off into the fire, and going about his business! His arm didn't swell up, and he seemed utterly unaffected by this terrible event! The locals decided that Paul must be a "god."

And they weren't so far wrong, really. Paul wasn't a god—but he was a true *son of God,* and he had the power of God operating in him, even in his own physical body! He knew his authority in Jesus—and he exercised it.

I looked again at what Jesus said through Mark: He was talking about *physical,* as well as spiritual, health and well-being. He was promising us that if serpents attacked us, or if we inadvertently or unavoidably took in poisons of some kind, we could use His Name and not be harmed! What an incredible promise! But would it work in the twentieth century—on a *flu bug?*

I discovered, firsthand, that Jesus "is the same yesterday, and to day, and for ever" (Hebrews 13:8), and that His Word and His Name and His authority still pack the same wallop they did in Paul's day.

I knew I couldn't avoid contact with those mysterious little poisonous creatures; they're *everywhere.* We take them into our bodies without even knowing it, until they've done their foul work. So I began something I continue to this day: I start the day thanking Jesus for a healthy body and asking Him, by His Spirit, to *keep* me strong, physically, mentally, and spiritually.

And He does it!

I have to do my part, though. First, I try to eat right, and to get at least a minimum amount of rest, and I take vitamins—all the normal health things. And when I feel a virus trying to establish a foothold, to get my body to raise a white flag and give up to its vicious onslaught—I get out my Bible, and I get on my knees and I take the offensive! I rebuke Satan's demonic plans, and I deliberately ask the Great Physician to inject my system with His precious Blood, that has already grappled with every sickness the Devil ever invented and whipped it! (*See* 1 Peter 2:24.) Peter says that Jesus offers us healing through what He suffered, and I believe that means healing for physical *and* spiritual diseases—because they both come from the same satanic infection. So I ask my Doctor, my Jesus, for a fresh "inoculation" of His healing Blood; and then, like Peter, I go about my business.

I think constant good health is a miracle, especially in this day of contamination, pollution, anxiety, and just plain old feverish demonic attack. But it's a miracle the Lord *wants* us to experience. He said, ". . . I am come that they might have life, and that they might have it more abundantly" (John 10:10), and "It is the spirit that quickeneth; the flesh profiteth nothing: the words that I speak unto you, they are spirit, and they are life" (John 6:63).

I take vitamin C; but I credit liberal doses of Jesus' life-giving Word for my daily miracle of health.

26 AN ALCOHOLIC'S MIRACLE

There are nine million alcoholics in this country.

That means there are nine million individuals with a fatal disease, just as deadly and hopeless and destructive as muscular dystrophy or polio or cancer.

The nine million figure makes alcoholism the nation's number one health problem, its greatest drug problem, its greatest potential killer—really Public Enemy Number 1! Alcohol addiction breaks up more homes every year, causes more traffic accidents and fatalities, contributes to more loss of property (in the billions of dollars), and wastes more human resources than any other single illness—and nobody has an answer.

Except Jesus.

This is just one of the miracles I've seen the Physician from Nazareth perform in the life of a hopeless alcoholic.

I got a letter from a man named Gene that really touched me. He lived in Southern California, had been very successful in business, made a lot of money, had a wife and several children, and seemed to have the world by the tail. Then he started to drink.

The well-known process led from casual, social drinking to occasional "benders" to pretty steady "soaking." Because he was well established in business, though, it appeared he could handle this growing addiction without his world coming apart.

Wrong.

In his letter, he outlined the dissolving of his marriage, the breakup of his family, the gradual disintegration of his businesses—and finally bankruptcy and total disgrace.

Gene said Alcoholics Anonymous had helped him gain some control of his personal habits, and that now he could hold a job; but they couldn't put his fractured life back together again, and nobody could give him back his health, which was shaky at best. He said he'd been very depressed, actually thinking of suicide—when somebody gave him a copy of *A New Song*.

He could easily understand the crises in my life, and felt himself being drawn to the Lord by a desire to share my "Song." He wrote that he'd never been baptized—and wondered if he could be included among the next bunch to obey the Lord's command in our swimming pool, if we were still making it available in that way.

Well, I intended to call him right away, to assure him he'd be welcome. But many other things distracted me, and several weeks went by. One Friday, knowing that a number of new Christians were going to be baptized in our pool the next morning, I hunted for Gene's letter, found it, and called him.

He seemed stunned. I breezily told him that I'd meant to call him for several weeks, but had been busy with other things, and that if he still wanted to be baptized, the next morning would be fine with us.

Rather haltingly, he promised he'd be there, and thanked me for calling.

Sure enough, at ten the next morning, there were about forty folks around our pool on a brilliantly sunny Saturday, singing happy Jesus songs and rejoicing over what God was doing in all our lives. The ones being baptized were all young people, high-school and college age mainly, coming to that moment through home Bible studies and street ministries that had no access to church baptistries. (That, by the way, accounts for most of the three hundred plus baptisms in our pool—we haven't started a new church, as some have thought.)

Gene arrived, introduced himself and a young lady who came with him. He'd asked her to come because he had talked to her just a few minutes before I called him the previous afternoon, and had calmly announced to her then that he was about to take his own life!

She'd been his contact with AA, and he felt he wanted *somebody* to know he was dead, and why, and to have some personal instructions about the disposition of his body and few remaining possessions. She'd tried valiantly to talk him out of it, but when he hung up without revealing where he was, she knew that he meant what he said and—unless a miracle occurred—would be dead in an hour.

Because there was nothing else to do, she prayed. Desperately, she asked God to touch Gene someway, *somehow.*

At that moment, I was looking for his letter.

Gene said that when the phone rang, he thought that the young lady had been able to find him somehow and almost didn't answer! His mind was made up: There was absolutely no reason to live. There'd been a glimmer of hope after he read *A New Song,* and he thought he felt himself being drawn toward God. But he'd written that foolish letter to an entertainer he'd never met, telling him his intimate life story, and actually asked if he—an alcoholic stranger—could come over and be included in a personal celebration and worship service at the entertainer's home! What monumental gall! Had he really expected to get an answer to a letter like that? Did he really expect a busy celebrity to even respond, much less invite him over? Did he really, down deep, believe the Lord of heaven and earth was listening to a whiskey-soaked has-been like Gene? Of course not.

Still, he picked up the phone, expecting to tell the young lady from AA to forget it—and heard my voice, inviting him to come over and be baptized.

I'm sure you'll understand, as I do, what Gene meant when he said, "I felt I was hearing the voice of the Lord Himself." He knew, as I did, that the exquisite timing of this moment, the last-second rescue of a derelict's life, had not been humanly arranged. God Himself, infinitely loving and "not willing that any should perish," was surely speaking to Gene, using my willing but blissfully ignorant voice!

And he obeyed.

He'd called the young lady back, and invited her to join him—and only then learned that she'd been frantically praying for his miracle. How beautiful that the Lord was letting her know so quickly that her prayer was heard—and answered!

Gene was baptized that morning, along with twenty or so young kids, including a whole hard-rock singing group, most of whom were Jewish. They'd been terribly strung out on drugs, several of them heroin addicts, when one by one they'd met the Messiah. And their stories, grotesque and tragic as they were, diffused now in a radiant overflowing joy, told Gene that he was not alone, either in his past misery—or his new life.

In the same way, the Spirit helps us in our weakness. We do not know how we ought to pray, but the Spirit Himself intercedes for us with groans that words cannot express. And He who searches our hearts knows the mind of the Spirit, because the Spirit intercedes for the saints in accordance with God's will. And we know that in all things God works for the good of those who love him, *who have been called according to his purpose.*

See Romans 8:26–28

Gene lived only a few short months after that happy morning. The alcohol took its final toll, but there was a vital difference in Gene, his outlook on life, and in his daily relationship with the Lord during his remaining time. I'm thankful for that.

And I'm deeply grateful for another evidence of the intimate way Jesus hears and involves Himself in our sorrows and joys—and for the new light shining from passages like this:

Or don't you know that all of us who were baptized into Christ Jesus were baptized into his death? We were therefore buried with him through baptism into death in order that, just as Christ was raised from the dead through the glory of the Father, we too may live a new life.

If we have been united with him in his death, we will certainly also be united with him in his resurrection. For we know that our old self was crucified with him so that the body of sin might be rendered powerless, that we should no longer be slaves to sin—because anyone who has died has been freed from sin.

Now if we died with Christ, we believe that we will also live with him.

Romans 6:3–8 NIV

27 GOOD VIBES

I'd like to share something with you that may be very hard for you to accept or understand. I don't "understand" it, myself!

Just yesterday, Lindy (our eighteen-year-old beauty) drove into the gas station after a half-hour wait. She didn't get out of the car. She just asked the attendant to fill the tank, and she waited.

Off to one side, waiting while their own tank was being filled, stood two young men, talking.

Lindy glanced in their direction a couple of times, and once her eyes met the gaze of one of the young men. She looked away with a pleasant smile, realizing she didn't know either of the guys—and that was that.

The attendant made out her bill, Lindy paid it, and started the engine to leave.

As she was rolling up her window, the young man who'd been looking at her said, "I sure love Jesus!"

Lindy did sort of a double take. This *was* Beverly Hills, wasn't it? There were no "Jesus stickers" on her car, and she was certain she'd never seen either of these two young men before, and that they couldn't know who she was or anything about her. And yet they were smiling warmly at her, proclaiming their love for Jesus, like old friends!

"So do I," she beamed.

Again, the same young man spoke. "Yes, I know."

Lindy just *had* to ask, ". . . but how?"

His reply came with a warm, even smile, "We have the same Spirit."

And Lindy drove away, bathed in goose bumps.

Strange, isn't it?

Almost—well, almost—supernatural, isn't it?

I believe it *is* supernatural, in the best sense, and I love it!

Young people today talk so much about "vibes"—vibrations—good and bad feelings that they get about people and situations. "Man, I really get good vibes from that dude . . . ," or "The whole scene gives off bad vibes." They're referring both to the subtle impression a person may create by his manner and actions—and to an inner intuitive response on the part of people around him.

There are several examples of this kind of "spiritual radar" in the New Testament. In Acts 4:13, the angry and frightened religious leaders who had arrested Peter and John for preaching about the Messiah ". . . took knowledge of them, that they had been with Jesus"! They knew—they could tell!

The disciples who actually walked with Jesus, without physically recognizing Him, on the road to Emmaus (Luke 24), said later after "their eyes were opened" (v. 31), *"Did not our heart burn within us, while He talked with us by the way?"* (V. 32, italics mine.)

They were literally picking up Jesus' "vibes"!

How is this possible? By a *spiritual* operation, a supernatural work of the Holy Spirit on the inner man. Paul says, "Now we have received, not the spirit of the world, but *the spirit which is of God;* that we might know the things that are freely given to us of God" (*see* 1 Corinthians 2:12). In that same chapter, verse 16, Paul adds, "We have the *mind of Christ*"!

What does that mean? Well, among other things, it means we should find developing within us the kind of spiritual discernment Jesus showed us in countless passages like Matthew 22:18, Luke 5:22, 20:23 and Mark 2:8—where He *"perceived"* the thoughts, intents, and motivations of others.

Mark says, "Jesus perceived in his spirit"; it was *not* an intellectual insight.

Paul adds that "the natural man receiveth not the things of the Spirit of God: for they are foolishness unto him: *neither can he know them— because they are spiritually discerned"* (1 Corinthians 2:14, italics mine).

I'm not saying we are supposed to reach a point where we can declare who is actually a Christian and who isn't; that's a dangerous game, and I don't want to play it.

But I do believe the Lord will give us some inner indications, in the Spirit, when we are with fellow believers—and perhaps some "warning signals" when we have companied with deceivers, or the deceived. And as the last days count down to their inevitable conclusion, and as we find ourselves swept onto a battlefield where *supernatural weapons* will become commonplace (*as they will*), each of us will need this spiritual gift; "For there shall arise false Christs, and false prophets, and shall show great signs and wonders; insomuch that, if it were possible, *they shall deceive the very elect*"! (*See* Matthew 24:24.)

What will make the difference? What will protect the "elect" from this fatal deception?

I believe it will be an expanded sensitivity in individual believers to the Spirit of God, coupled with a deep knowledge of His Word.

What happened to Lindy at the service station was just a hint, a beautiful preview.

After all, shouldn't Jesus in me recognize Jesus in you when we meet?

---

1 John 5:7–10

28   GOD LIVES AT MAMA AND DADDY'S HOUSE

He that has my commandments, and keepeth them, he it is that loveth me: and he that loveth me shall be loved of my Father, and I will love him, and *will manifest myself to him.*

Judas saith unto him, not Iscariot, Lord, how is it that thou wilt manifest thyself unto *us,* and not unto the world?

Jesus answered and said unto him, If a man love me, he will keep my words: and my Father will love him, and *we will come unto him, and make our abode with him.*

See John 14:21–23

Now I suppose that you would concede a miracle had happened, if one day you heard a knock at your door, you opened it—and saw standing in brilliant shimmering sunbursts of light two heavenly Beings, One of whom said, "Hello. I'm Jehovah God, and this is My Son, Jesus. We've come to live with you—may We come in?"

I'm really not trying to be funny; if you read Jesus' own words in John 14, you can't escape some kind of mental picture of just such an eventuality. He *says*, "We will come to him, We will manifest ourselves, make Our presence undeniable, *dwell* with him!"

What in the world did Jesus mean?

Surely He didn't mean exactly what He said—did He?

He did.

But the key is in Judas's obvious question: "Lord, how will You make Your Presence unmistakable to people who love You and keep Your commandments—and at the same time still be hidden to those who don't love and believe You?"

It is a puzzle, and Jesus meant it to be. He answered Judas by assuring him that God would greatly love the individual who sets his *heart*—not just his mind—to believe and obey Him, and that Jesus and His Father would come and dwell intimately with that individual!

I've had so many people, especially Christians, ask me, "Sure, that sounds great, and I guess I sort of believe it, but—how can you *know* that God is pleased with you, and how can you really *know* that He's dwelling with you?"

The question is right out on the table, and terrible in its implication. The question really is: Can the God of heaven and earth, the Being who wouldn't allow Moses to see Him in His awesome power lest Moses be consumed, the One who spoke all things into existence, *live in my house without my even knowing He's around?*

Can this mighty God, and the Lord Jesus Himself, dwell in my body and not make Their Presence obvious, even to *me?*

Not likely, friend. Not likely.

Remember, we're talking about the Person who descended upon Mount Sinai "in fire: its smoke ascended like that of a furnace, and the whole mountain quaked greatly!" (*See* Exodus 19:18.) And "all the people perceived the thunderings and the lightnings and the noise of the trumpet and the smoking mountain, and as they looked they trembled with fear, and fell back and stood afar off. And they said to Moses, You speak to us, and we will listen, *but let not God speak to us, lest we die!*" (*See* Exodus 20:18, 19.)

We're talking about the One whose power is so immense that when King Solomon invited Him to come dwell in the newly constructed temple, "the house of the Lord was filled with a cloud, So that the priests could not stand to minister because of the cloud; for *the glory of the Lord filled the house of God*"! (*See* 2 Chronicles 5:13, 14.)

No, this is not your usual house guest!

Jesus, through God's miracles, condensed His own Second-Person grandeur into a human body, but even then He had such fearsome power that demonic armies trembled before Him, the wind and the waves obeyed His voice, the dead came from the tomb, and Satan himself backed away. The armed soldiers who came to arrest Him in the garden "fell backward to the ground" when He said simply, "I am he" (John 18:6). At the moment of Jesus' death, when the earth shook mightily, the rocks split, the graves opened and the dead came tumbling out *alive*— the Roman centurion and those with him "feared greatly, saying, Truly this was the Son of God" (Matthew 27:54).

This Man was no shrinking violet, no milk toast, no wallflower. When He was around, you *knew* it!

When He went to Zaccheus's house (Luke 19), this rich and unscrupulous tax collector *changed!* Right away! As he was exposed to the presence of God's Son in his own home, Zaccheus felt his own unworthiness and began to pledge himself to a new way of life; and Jesus joyfully acknowledged, "Today salvation is come to your house" (*see* v. 9).

There was no guesswork—something had happened!

When the two disciples walked with Jesus on the road to Emmaus (Luke 24), they didn't recognize Him physically. They were too sure He was dead, and were wrapped in their own self-pity. But after Jesus sat down to bread with them, and after He dwelt intimately with them for a short time, *"Their eyes were opened, and they recognized Him . . ."* (*see* v. 31). And when He'd left them, they said to one another, *"Didn't our hearts burn within us,* while He talked with us along the way, and while He opened to us the Scriptures?" (*See* v. 32.)

Oh, yes—His Presence will always be felt.

But in answer to Judas's question, His Presence will be felt *by those whose hearts open to Him,* while others nearby may remain oblivious to the fact that the Son of God is in their midst!

What happened to my own Mama and Daddy is a beautiful example.

My parents have always been wonderful people, honest and hardworking, open and generous, regular and devout churchgoers. Daddy has been a Sunday-school teacher ever since I can remember, a deacon, and eventually an elder in the Church of Christ. He's a building contractor, and in fact, his company built the magnificent structure that houses the congregation we called our church home for many years. Mama's a registered nurse and a real "get-involved" lady, always in the thick of the church, scout, and school activities.

Our family was always at church every time the doors were open, and usually right up front! The Bible was open at our house, and we really tried to be good church members and real Christians.

So, when Shirley and I began to tell Mama and Daddy about the miracles we were experiencing, and about the "Baptism in the Holy Spirit," and talking about Jesus as if He actually *lived* and *talked* with us—well, Daddy began to study his Bible all the *more,* to "straighten us out"!

But funny thing—the more Daddy studied, looking up all the references to the Holy Spirit in the Bible (a monumental task; He's on practically every page!) and trying to make all he was learning fit into our rigid church doctrine, the more *questions* he had—not answers! Gradually, over a period of some months, he came to his own conclusion that Christians really were settling for far less than God wanted them to have. It was precisely our doctrinal judgments that were cutting us off from God's rich provision, blinding us to the gifts He was holding out to every believer.

Still, even after he'd decided that our experiences were valid and real for *us*—after all, he'd seen an unexplainable new glow about my family, a flowing charged-up zeal for the Bible and for Jesus—he wasn't sure this Holy Spirit Baptism was for him and Mama. They'd done fine for many years without it, hadn't they? Still . . . .

He went to a Full Gospel Business Men's meeting in Nashville.

This was a frequent happening in almost every city in America, and informal gathering of successful businessmen in every field, where newcomers were encouraged to "get acquainted with God, the Holy Spirit," introduced by enthusiastic men whose own lives had been changed and enriched through intimate encounters with Him. But, though Daddy was favorably impressed with the zeal and obvious spiritual power in the meeting, he went home more doubtful about the likelihood of something like that happening to him. There was an emotional pitch—an open fervency about the gathering that was just foreign to him.

He was a building contractor, a practical man who had to fully analyze a situation and see its risks and disadvantages as well as its potential. He'd always maintained a good grip on his emotions and was frankly afraid of getting swept into some phony or shallow spiritual "trip."

He spoke this concern to the Lord, and he and Mama asked Him to fill them completely with His Spirit. They believed He had more for each of them, but they would trust Him to administer His gifts to them personally.

And He did!

One quiet early morning, soon after they'd uttered that prayer, Daddy was going about his long-established morning routine, fixing his own breakfast, and shaving and reading his Bible while Mama slept, when it happened. He closed his Bible and dropped to his knees to pray. He wasn't asking for anything; actually, he was thanking the Lord for all His countless goodnesses, as he thought about his four healthy kids and their mates, and all the grandchildren, and Mama and his business—and a feeling of gratitude, of inexpressible joy, rose quickly within him. He said later that he'd experienced the feeling before, during prayer, but like most men, he didn't know how to vocalize that intense joyful feeling, so he'd choked it off. Literally. And a feeling of joy had turned to a feeling of pain, of constriction in the throat.

But not this morning.

No, this morning, when that sudden happy response to God rose inside him, Daddy just allowed it to pour out! Instead of stifling it, he kept on praying, but without groping desperately for words. He heard himself uttering a fluid, very expressive language which he knew was praise and thanksgiving—though he didn't recognize any of the words! He was speaking, *and the Holy Spirit was shaping the utterance,* exactly like Acts 2:4! It was glorious.

Several minutes went by this way, and then all was still.

Daddy looked around.

It was still the same quiet morning, everything around him quite ordinary—Mama hadn't even waked up!

Was it this simple, this contact with God, this praying in the Spirit? It was. Jesus had manifested Himself to Daddy, right in his normal morning routine, intimately but very definitely.

Later, as Daddy made the rounds between his company's jobs, he prayed as he drove. To his delight, he found that the Lord was traveling with him, listening to him and supernaturally shaping his "prayer language," the Spirit actually praying with him as He promised He would in Romans 8:26!

It *wasn't* an emotional "trip"! Oh, his emotions were stirred, they were involved; but it was deeper, sweeter than that. It was truly a *spiritual* experience, a happening in his "inner man." What Paul said was *true:* "For if I pray in an [unknown] tongue, my spirit [by the Holy Spirit within me] prays, but my mind is unproductive—bears no fruit and helps nobody" (1 Corinthians 14:14, AMPLIFIED). His intellect wasn't directing this part of his prayer; it wasn't really contributing or limiting it—but his *heart* "burned within him," like those two disciples on the road to Emmaus.

Daddy was learning what it was to be in the Presence of Jesus!

Naturally, Mama was thrilled; and she knew now that someday soon Jesus would manifest Himself to her.

She didn't have long to wait.

A few days later, again in the early morning, she was sleeping while Daddy was going about his usual routine. Mama had always had vivid dreams, but *this* morning's was the winner of all time! In her dream, she saw a clear blue sky, pristine and sparkling. Way off in the distance, she saw a tiny cloud coming, and growing as it drifted her way. As she watched, it was joined by other clouds, and soon her vision was completely filled with thick, white clouds, becoming turbulent and churning with life. Something tremendous and climactic was about to happen; the whole sky was boiling and about to explode—and *suddenly* the clouds burst apart, opening in a flash and rolling back. In a brilliant explosion of dazzling light, a majestic figure was looming toward her with outstretched hands, a radiant smile on His divine face, approaching her from above with the speed and grace and beauty of light—it was *Jesus!*

In her dream, Mama raised her hands in awe and joyous welcome to this fast-approaching Messiah, and from her heart sprang spontaneous praise, rippling from her innermost being and pouring from her lips—and in that instant, she was awake! She was sitting up, trembling, no longer seeing Jesus with her eyes, but still so aware of His Presence, and the praise was still pouring from her—but now it was in whispers of love and adoration, mingled with tears of joy running freely down her cheeks.

She doesn't know to this day how many minutes she praised the Lord this way, but in a little bit Daddy came in and asked gently, "Margaret, it's happened, hasn't it?"

She nodded, wiping the tears away.

Daddy said he hadn't heard anything, but in his prayers in the other room, he'd suddenly been aware that something was happening with Mama. He got up and came in—to find that Jesus had manifested Himself to her, just as he'd promised He'd do for every believer who would "keep his words" and seek Him in His fullness.

And His manifestations were so unique, so tailored to their individual personalities, as personal as their fingerprints. They were perfect demonstrations of the *love* of a Father who knows us each so well, so intimately. And they explained the mystery Judas was trying to understand when he asked, "How can you manifest yourself to *us*—and not to the world?"

Mama and Daddy have changed a lot since those precious days.

They were "good" before but they're different now. They radiate a love and warmth and compassion that is deeper and fuller and wiser; people of all ages are drawn to that "special something" in Archie and Margaret Boone. They eat and drink and *live* that living Word, and minister its strength and reality to hungry, searching, troubled people around them every day. It's so beautiful—it's so real!

Oh, they were eventually "disfellowshiped," declared no longer members, in their longtime home church (just like the blind man Jesus touched in John 9; he was cast out of the synagogue by the frightened religious leaders who couldn't understand this manifestation of Jesus' power, because what had happened to them didn't fit the accepted doctrine of their brethren). But Mama and Daddy still sit in the same pew at most of the services there, in the magnificent building Daddy built, though now they're considered visitors—not members.

And they love all those good folks around them just the same, even *more* than before, because now they're experiencing the love of God that ". . . is shed abroad in our hearts by the Holy Spirit which is given to us" (Romans 5:5). They understand completely the suspicion, the doubt, the scepticism, the honest concern of their brethren—because they've been there.

But they're growing all the time in the Word, in grace, and in the Spirit—because God has come to live at Mama and Daddy's house.

29 MIRACLE OF THE WITCH

Mr. and Mrs. Arnold Green
announce the marriage in Christ
of their daughter
Sara
to
Douglas Binkley
Sunday, June fourteenth
nineteen hundred and seventy-four
at two o'clock
Prince of Peace Lutheran Church

This was the text of a wedding invitation I received not long ago. I guess everybody has seen one or more of these, and I've seen hundreds. But this one moved me quickly to tears, even though I've never seen any of the people named in it. This was unlike any wedding invitation I'd ever received—because of the story behind it.

I knew the prospective bride had been a witch!

I mean a real, dedicated Satan-worshiping witch—the kind they used to burn at the stake! A twenty-two-year-old girl who had given her soul to the Devil!

I shivered a little when I got the first letter from this girl Sara (this obviously is not her real name). You may shiver some, too.

Read it:

Dear Pat:

I know you don't know me, but please don't let that stop you from reading this. I need your advice.

Maybe I should introduce myself. My name is Sara Green. I'm 21 years old. For three years I was a witch, but from there I went into Satan worship. I practiced black magic, drank blood and urine, ate flesh, praised Satan, and conjured up demons. Satan was my Lord and I loved him. I had relations with animals for a while. I wanted to be a high priestess. I thought I could be one sooner if I destroyed your work. I read your book *A New Song* to find out where your weak points were. I didn't find any, but the book really affected me. I knew you were writing about something real, and I wanted it.

Well, after reading the book I wanted Jesus. My old associates knew and started threatening, so I moved. They hate Christians.

I tried to pray to Jesus, but it seemed like a civil war started inside. Gods argued inside of me. Demons showed up. I don't know what happened, but every time I started to pray I couldn't. I can't figure anything out. I don't know why I can't pray.

I sometimes have suicide thoughts. I can't understand it, because I don't want to die. Could you help? Is there anything I should be doing?

I can't go inside a church. I usually get convulsions then. What am I doing wrong? Why can't I pray? Is there any hope? I'm writing sort of freely. I'd like to get everything out.

I know you get a lot of mail, so I don't know whether this will get to you or not. If you ever have time, though, could you maybe write? I'd really appreciate any advice.

Sincerely yours,
SARA GREEN

What would *you* have done next?

Throw the letter away—burn it? Turn it over to the police, or to a minister or priest? Would you pray for your own protection?

I did.

Nobody had to tell me I was in a new tug-of-war, a real nitty-gritty skirmish with demonic forces, and there was terrific danger in it. I prayed for the covering of the Blood of Jesus, and for guidance of the Holy Spirit in reaching out to this poor victim of Satan's all-out conquest of the human race.

Does it surprise you that a healthy young girl from a Christian background would volunteer her life, her body, her very soul to Satan—in the twentieth century? in America, the "churchiest" country in the world? It shouldn't.

Did you think that the Charles Manson slaughter rampage (in which Sharon Tate and others were butchered by young kids who really believed Charlie was "Christ" *and* the devil) was a unique happening? Have you missed the connection between that horror and a real Devil?

Have you been mystified about the root cause of unthinkable violence like the Zebra killings, the SLA, the constant bombings and killing in Ireland, the Maalot massacre of children—and countless other soul-searing tragedies that will happen by the time you read this?

Has it occurred to you there might be some connection between the rapid increase in rapes and other violent crimes in America, and the fantastic new involvement with the occult and witchcraft and outright Satan worship in our country? *Time* magazine, in its June 19, 1972 issue which featured an in-depth look at the occult in the United States, with a picture of an actual Satan worshiper on the cover and the headline SATAN RETURNS, stated that there are already thousands of witches in America today! (It's not really known how many.) And it's spreading like wildfire, with covens forming in high schools in every city, and the Satanic Bible outselling the Holy Bible on thousands of college campuses—it's the *in* thing!

The Rolling Stones are just one of the major rock groups that sing often about his satanic majesty in rock hymns like "Sympathy for the Devil" and whole albums like *Goat's Head Soup*. In fact, it was *while* this particular group was singing "Sympathy for the Devil" for over 300 thousand fans at Altamont Raceway in California that violence and death erupted in the frenzied crowd. Coincidence?

No, it's real. Evil is real. Sin is real. Satan is real.

And those who worship Satan and align themselves with occult and mystic and demonic forces are dealing with *reality!* A great part of the tragedy is that many, many folks who dabble in the occult and hidden forms of satanic practices think they're playing some kind of "game." They really think they can participate for a while in exciting devil games, and when they get bored, move on to some other so-called trip. They really are mystified (blinded) as to why they can't get their lives together again afterwards—ever!

They actually don't quite believe the Devil is real, even after they've worshiped him! But that shouldn't seem so odd, really; too many "religious" people aren't sure of *God's* reality, even after years of church-going. It's highly unfashionable today, in many churches, to talk about God *or* Satan as much more than "concepts." So much more sophisti-cated, more adult, more urbane and reasonable and intellectually attrac-tive, to discuss good and evil in the abstract!

All of this, while *Time* reports that *three million West Germans to-day are involved somehow in the occult. It's been said, too, there are more witches in England right now than priests, that the Catholic church in Italy and around the world is being forced to reactivate its theology and training in exorcism, to combat the alarming rise in witchcraft and demon possession*—and ritual murders, animal sacrifices, and desecration of sacred sites are on the increase—*and "adult" bookstores and direct-mail companies are panting to meet the demand for more information on the occult, worldwide!*

I was in Spokane, Washington, just a couple of years ago, during the week that Mont St. Michael, a Catholic monastery, was given to Teen Challenge because only eighteen applicants had applied for priesthood that year—and *that same week,* the local newspaper reported that local Church of Satan had ordained four hundred new "ministers"! Who in

his right mind would want to be a minister in the Church of Satan?
Good question.

(1) Businessmen—tax advantages, in any "church"
(2) Housewives—exciting relief from boredom
(3) College kids—license to do all the things most churches forbid,
    plus drug involvement

Friends of mine in San Antonio, Detroit, Minneapolis, Nashville,
New Orleans, and Toronto have been shocked to find out that their own
kids are fully aware of the witches' covens in their own high schools—
and some have already been drawn into them!

But I've got news for *Time* magazine: *Satan hasn't "returned"—he's
never been away!* He's just coming out into the open, encouraging the
vast, spiritually starved world to fall down and worship him!

So, after a lot of prayer, thought and study in the Word, I wrote
Sara. The letter may seem long, but I hope you'll read every line; it
was a vital part of this miracle, and you may just need to know some of
this yourself:

Dear Sara:
I'm very, very sorry that a month has gone by since you wrote me your
letter. I was out of town with my family on a concert tour until barely
a week ago. Naturally, since I've been gone almost six weeks, I'm much
behind in my mail.

I'm quite sure, though, that the Lord heard your cry and has kept you
safe until now. It may be that He's already answered your questions and
drawn you into a warm Christian fellowship by now—but in the event
that He has given me the opportunity to help you, I want to give you my
prayerful response to your letter.

What you felt as you read *A New Song* is real. This is the combined call
of your own soul and of the Holy Spirit of God together. And, Sara, let
me give you this encouragement: no power in heaven or earth, or under
the earth, can overcome that team! Once your soul combines with the Holy
Spirit in earnest desire, Satan himself and all of his legions cannot overcome
you! *Please read immediately Romans 8:31 through 39.*

I hope you have a Bible near by, and that you have access to a modern
translation of some kind. I certainly recommend The Living Bible, or the

Good News for Modern Man: in fact, I think I'll send one with this letter. God's Word is your most powerful weapon. Even when you don't *feel* anything you can believe God to perform exactly what He says He will do. So it's very important that you have a Bible handy, and I would really recommend that you carry it with you all the time for a while. *Remember:* Jesus met Satan face-to-face in the wilderness (Matthew 4:1–11). He brought no weapon with him except the Word of God! When He said, "It is written . . ." three separate times, it was like bludgeoning Satan with an atomic hammer. The Devil knows God's Word, and has to respect and obey it when a believer speaks it.

Please read Ephesians 6:10 through 18. This passage tells us exactly what the nature of the battle is, and what our weapons are. You may not understand all of this right now, but at least I'm sure God will give you an understanding of the nature of the battle and how much He loves you and how He has already given you everything you need to win the battle. In fact, He's fighting on your side! Let your heart rejoice with this knowledge!

Did you ever see a tag wrestling match? This is when there are at least two wrestlers on each team, and only one from each team is allowed to wrestle in the ring at any one time. When one wrestler is getting badly beaten by his opponent, if he can just get back to his corner, or even close enough to reach out and touch the fingertips of his partner (in other words, if he can tag him), his partner can immediately leap into the ring, drag off the opponent who has the upper hand, and take over the battle himself! The partner who is being beaten can then drag himself off the floor and outside the ropes and rest and recuperate—*while his fresh strong partner takes up the battle.*

Sara, we are in a tag-team scrap with the Devil and his angels. You have been out in the center of the ring, and in fact, over in the Devil's corner, and have been getting the daylights beaten out of you. In fact, I guess, you didn't even know you were in a battle because you willingly joined his team. Now that you have begun to scrap, and have tried to get back into the other corner, he is certainly going to put up a fight, and drag you back if he can. He will use old friends, he will use his demons, he will accuse you and try to stand between you and Jesus in every way he can. The old suicide trick is one of his favorites. If he can't keep you willingly on his side, then he'll try to convince you that you've lost the battle, there's no reason to live, and that you should end it all. Then he's got you forever. Because you have allowed him to have control of your body, and get his hooks in you, he will exert every possible influence to keep you from touching Jesus. He has the ability to give you physical pain, emotional and spiritual obstacles, to work through friends and even family to block your path. He knows (even better than you or I) that if you simply reach out and touch the tip of Jesus' finger—he's had it! Jesus will come bounding over those ropes and scatter him right out of your life!

Here is the most important part of this letter: Read these verses in chapter 10 of Romans. Begin with verse 9 and read through 11. These verses simply say that Jesus is as near to you as your own mouth! To touch Him, and bring Him into the battle, all you have to do is speak His Name! As you speak His Name—*Jesus* (which means *Jehovah is our salvation*)—and believe in your heart that He *is* the Son of God, and ask Him to come into your life and to be your Lord and your Saviour, He will! In verse 10, God Himself says that "with the mouth confession is made unto salvation"! Can it be simpler than that? Satan himself cannot prevent you from speaking that Name, receiving your salvation, and bringing Jesus and His Father into the battle for your life. Now read verse 13 and do it!

Don't put it off for even a second. The Devil will try to stop you; he may threaten you physically; he may try to convince you that your heart will stop or your brain will explode, or that your tongue simply will not speak that Name. But, Sara, God is on your side, or I would not have received this letter. And you would not be reading this answer right now.

One last example. Remember the thief on the cross? Here Jesus was already nailed to the cross and His life's blood was draining away. On one side of Him was a thief who recognized that Jesus really was the Son of God. He was already nailed to a similar cross for his own sins. Even in that lost, dying, and hopeless situation, he simply turned and spoke to Jesus and recognized Him as the Son of God. Jesus turned and said to him, "This day you shall be with me in paradise." Your situation cannot be as hopeless as that poor thief on the cross. And Jesus saved him and took him that day to paradise! Isn't that thrilling? This is in Luke 23:39 through 43.

Sara, I'm praying right now that Jesus will get this letter to you quickly, that He will make the Bibles available to you, and that He will bring Christian friends into your life who have the power and the knowledge of the Holy Spirit operating in them. I believe He'll do this. Will you cooperate by doing a strange thing? Will you fast—go without food—for a day or two or three? In chapter 4 of the little Book of James, God says in verses 7 and 8 that if you resist the Devil, he must flee from you. He also says that if you will draw near to God *He will draw near to you!*

One of the very best ways to draw n̄ar to God is to deny your flesh, to actually go without food for a tim̄ and let every hunger pang be a silent prayer for the Lord to draw neaı to you. He will! Jesus actually fasted for forty days before He met the Devil in that big showdown. None of us could do that; but if you will make that your prayer for a day or two or three, I earnestly believe that the Lord Himself will bring into your life Spirit-filled believers who will minister to you, and take you out of the influence of Satan and those that he still dominates. Do not believe that you can't pray! *Your letter itself is a prayer.* Your fasting will be a prayer. And every word you speak that is directed to the Lord is a prayer. Don't believe that because you don't feel you're getting through that you're not. You *are*—this letter proves it!

One last Scripture in this spiritual prescription: read Lamentations (in the Old Testament between Jeremiah and Ezekiel), chapter 3, verses 22–28. Also read verses 40 and 41. These have a description of where *you've* been, but also of the goodness and ever ready mercy of God. He loves you and is already working to answer the prayers that you didn't think were getting through! Be happy, Sara! Write me and let me know the good news. I'm praying for you *now*—and I know that the Lord has already engineered your salvation and a life of happy relationship with Him. Write me the good news.

> In the love of Jesus,
> PAT BOONE

Are you still with me?

Sara was.

And so was the good Lord. Jesus gave this earnest young lady the inner strength to fast and pray and read that precious Bible. He caused Christian young people to "just happen" across her path, and drew her into a Jesus fellowship. One of the young men who was especially attracted to her was Doug, who'd had his *own* fearful battles with demonic power and had learned firsthand the victory that is in Jesus alone. As he ministered to Sara, the Lord drew these two refugees from the satanic wars together.

The invitation to their marriage—in Christ—brought the tears to my eyes, and does again, right now. What a miracle!

It wasn't easy for Doug and Sara; the old witches' coven threatened them both with death, and the Devil won't take this defeat lying down.

But they're not afraid. They're on *God's* side now, and they know who *wins* this war.

They're trusting God, and Paul says, "God is faithful, who will not [permit] you to be tempted [tested] beyond your ability, but will with the temptation [trial] also make the way to escape, so that you may be able to bear it" (*see* 1 Corinthians 10:13).

And through the Baptism in the Holy Spirit, they've followed Paul's direct admonition:

Last of all I want to remind you that your strength must come from *the Lord's mighty power within you.* Put on all of God's armor so that you will be able to stand safe against all strategies and tricks of Satan. For we are not fighting against people made of flesh and blood, but *against persons without bodies* . . . the great evil princes of darkness *who rule this world;* and against huge numbers of wicked spirits in the spirit world. So *use every piece of God's armor* to resist the enemy whenever he attacks, and when it is all over, you will still be standing up.

Ephesians 6:10–13 LB (italics mine)

Are you still doubtful about miracles and supernatural gifts of God? Tell me—who else could have turned a witch into a saint?

30   MIRACLE IN THE AIR

How are you at flying?

I don't mean to dig up that terrible old joke, "I just flew in from Chicago—and boy, are my arms tired!"

I mean, if and when you fly in an airplane, can you relax and enjoy it? Do you just sit back and revel in the luxury, the *miracle* of modern air travel, eating the food that's brought, reading a magazine, and gazing with awe and delight at the passing landscapes thirty thousand feet below?

Or are you a "white-knuckle" flyer?

Are there giant butterflies already airborne in your stomach three days before *you* take off? Is there a feeling of controlled panic in your breast as the stewardess closes the EXIT door? Do you have to tranquilize yourself with pills or booze before, during, and after the flight? Do you secretly grip the seat till your hands turn white, and then green? Is there a deep feeling of dread that you'll never see your loved ones again; does a vivid picture keep flashing through your mind of the plane you're in hurtling toward the ground—till you wish you'd never planned the trip?

At every bump or air pocket, do you wish you'd increased your insurance? While you're in the air, do you learn what it is to "pray without ceasing"?

Then this miracle is for *you*.

My wife, Shirley, was in that second category all her life, till Jesus changed her. She was a real white-knuckle flyer, nervous and apprehensive for days before flight time, constantly looking for reasons she shouldn't go at all. She'd *never* fly alone, and yet was frightened for us to travel together, picturing our daughters with nobody to bring them up. The only solution was not to fly at all—and that's what she did, whenever it was possible.

Lots of entertainers are like that; some of the biggest stars of all have *never* flown! And many, many of the rest go by train or boat whenever possible, even passing up terrific career opportunities if flying is involved. Others—entertainers and athletes and business people who absolutely *have* to fly—spend thousands on psychiatrists and hypnotists and gurus (and pharmacists and distillers) so that they can handle the uncontrollable fear that wells up in them at the thought of leaving the ground.

Stewardesses report that their biggest problem is handling folks who get absolutely potted in the air—and yet they know that it's *fear* that causes the passengers to drink, and without the alcoholic "pain-killer" most of them couldn't (or wouldn't) dare to fly. Sad, but true.

Well, Shirley never drank to escape her fear—she just lived with it!

And so did the rest of us, because fear and anxieties have an infectious quality that communicates to others, breeding irritability and short tempers and even physical discomforts.

But in her book, *One Woman's Liberation,* she describes the turning point in her spiritual life, her encounter with Jesus as Baptizer in the Holy Spirit. In intimate detail, she shares the disintegraton of our life together and her own rising insecurity and loss of identity that brought her near to suicide. She describes how her desperate frustrations and inner vacuum led her to prayer and the Bible—and to Jesus.

Tortured by feelings of inadequacy and failure, and fearing she'd even lost her capacity to love, she dropped to her knees in our bedroom, alone, and asked the Lord to take over her life completely, to cleanse her of all her soul-stains, and to fill her with Himself, to baptize her in His own Holy Spirit.

And He did—right then!

Though you really can't describe such a moment adequately, she says that when she'd said everything she could think of in English, expressing her deep need and her hunger for the touch of Jesus, *she continued to offer him the sound of her voice,* praying that the Lord would accept her poor offering and fashion it into a miracle of praise, according to the promise and example of passages like John 1:33; Mark 16:17; Acts 2:4; 10:44–47; Romans 8:26, 27, and 1 Corinthians 14:2.

Shirley realized that *forty-five minutes* had been consumed with praise and adoration! She couldn't even have imagined such a thing before—and it left such an "afterglow" of peace and well-being.

Now, friend, as wonderful (or impossible) as this sounds, it didn't stop there.

I hadn't *had* this Baptism in the Holy Spirit experience, and neither had anybody else in my whole family; it would be at least six months before I came to my own encounter with Jesus as Baptizer. And though Shirley told me all about it, I had so many questions and doctrinal reservations and personal inhibitions that I might *never* have asked the Lord to fill me in the same way—*if I hadn't seen my wife change before my eyes into a different kind of woman!*

The Shirley I'd come to know—a volatile, changeable, up-and-down emotional chameleon—an increasingly troubled, anxious, insecure, nervous, and physical wreck—was transformed day by day into a stable, confident, secure, warm, and loving person, healthy and giving and quietly ready for any of life's crises! It was amazing, it was impossible— it was a *miracle!*

Humanly speaking, two very dramatic evidences proved that something supernatural had happened. First, I saw love in Shirley's eyes for *me*— love I had forfeited and lost, and had no real expectation of ever seeing again. Lost love is almost impossible to regain, and yet Shirley was drawing on some invisible Source—and seeing qualities in me I didn't know were there.

And second, I discovered *she'd lost her fear of flying!*

I say *I* discovered it, because she didn't seem to realize it! I was watching her very closely during the six months after her Baptism, and we flew a number of times in that period. There was *no fear,* no apprehension, no display of nerves, or even tension—before, during, or after a flight—no "white knuckles," no butterflies, no suppressed panic. It just didn't seem to *matter* to Shirley anymore whether she was on the ground or in the air!

I finally mentioned it to her one day after we took off and the pilot had turned off the SEAT BELT signs. Her eyes widened, she thought a second, and said, "You're right! I hadn't even thought about it. I'm not afraid anymore, not at all—praise the Lord!"

And that was that. Even when she consciously thought about the possibility of a crash, tried to picture the plane going down, even when we'd hit an air pocket or real rough weather, she said she felt like she was literally cradled in the hands of God—and unless He permitted it, *nothing* could force that plane off its course. So what was there to worry about?

That's a miracle.

You ask a psychiatrist if he can literally *take away a person's fear;* at best, he hopes to help the person live with it, adjust to it, control it. Ask a so-called positive thinker the same question; he'll try to help a person concentrate on something else, persuade himself he's *not* afraid. Ask a hypnotist; he'll try to get the person's subconscious to take over, and hide the fear from his *consciousness. None* of them can just take the fear away—for good.

Only God can do that.

Through Paul, the Lord advises, "And be not conformed to this world, but be transformed by the renewing of your mind . . ." (Romans 12:2).

But how in the world can a person have his or her mind re*newed?* You can have a tire recapped, a sofa recovered, a physical organ replaced, maybe. But a mind renewed? How?

Paul explained it to Timothy: *"For God hath not given us the spirit of fear; but of power, and of love, and of a sound mind"* (2 Timothy 1:7). He wrote to Titus: "Not by works of righteousness which we have done, but according to his mercy he saved us, by the washing of regeneration and *renewing of the Holy* [*Spirit*]; Which He shed on us abundantly through Jesus Christ our Saviour" (Titus 3:5, 6, italics mine).

Shirley *experienced* the absolute reality of this spiritual operation, as well as these words from the Apostle John: "There is no fear in love, but *perfect love casteth out fear:* because fear hath torment. He that feareth is not made perfect in love" (*see* 1 John 4:18).

And how do you come by this perfect love that casts out fear? Paul again: ". . . the love of God is shed abroad in our hearts *by the Holy* [*Spirit*] *which is given unto us"!* (*See* Romans 5:5.)

Shirley says that if she got on a plane and walked back to her seat—and found Jesus of Nazareth sitting in the seat next to hers, she'd feel pretty relaxed about the flight! How could you worry, sitting next to the Master of earth and sky, the One who stilled the wind and sea with a word? Wouldn't His Presence make *you* feel pretty secure?

Well, we both know that Jesus has His reservation on any flight we make, because He said, "Lo, I am with you alway, even unto the end of the world" (Matthew 28:20). Oh, if we'd only believe Him!

And why *don't* we believe Him? Paul hit it again; "But I fear, lest by any means, *as the serpent beguiled Eve through his* [*craftiness*], *so your minds should be corrupted* from the simplicity that is in Christ" (*see* 2 Corinthians 11:3).

See why we need miracles? Because we're in a supernatural struggle with a mightily endowed supernatural enemy, who intends to rob and destroy us! And we can't even *see* him, as Eve could, to defend ourselves!

There's only One who can see the Devil, and knows his plans—and He offers us supernatural assistance, with a 100 percent guarantee of victory! Shirley, in her simple, trusting way, obeyed Jesus' words in Matthew 6:33: "Seek ye first the kingdom of God, and his righteousness; and [everything you need will be given to you]"—and His assurance: "The Father knows what you need *before you ask*" (*see* Matthew 6:8) became real! She couldn't know the next few years would require *thousands* of miracles of her—but the Father did, and as she sought Him first, His love filled her and simply left no room for fear!

But we're making our reservations for *another* flight, another miracle in the air:

For the Lord himself shall descend from heaven with a shout, with the voice of the archangel, and with the trump of God: and the dead in Christ shall rise first: Then we who are alive and remain shall be caught up together with them *in the clouds, to meet the Lord in the air:* and so shall we ever be with the Lord. Wherefore, comfort one another with these words.

1 Thessalonians 4:16–18 (italics mine)

31   OF CRICKETS AND KINGS

I'm about to take a real gamble now.

The happening I want to share with you is intensely personal, and so very precious to me—one of the sweetest, most exciting moments of my life—but many will think this story is weird, implausible, happenstance, imagined, or that I've just plain flipped out.

I've decided to tell it, though, for two reasons:

(1) it really happened

(2) and I believe it's a glimpse of the way man was meant to live—
and *will,* when "that which is perfect is come" (1 Corinthians
13:10), when God has restored Creation to its original state and
man is in harmony with all other living things.

I was visiting my Mama and Daddy in Nashville, making an album,
and eating all that good home cooking. It was just after dinner on a
late spring evening—still daylight—and my folks had just pulled out of
the driveway on their way to one of the many Bible studies they're part
of each week. I'd been to several with them already, but this particular
night I elected to stay home, sit in the old porch swing and hide out.
At 8 o'clock I wanted to watch the debut of Julie Andrews's new series
on TV.

As I rocked gently back and forth in the porch swing, watching the
lightning bugs blink on and off in the gathering twilight, feeling that
wonderful warm, full sensation that sweeps over me every time I'm
home at our old place in Nashville, my thoughts swam with memories
of happy times, growing pains—Mama fixing my runny noses and broken
bones and bruised ego—Daddy trying to explain why we couldn't afford
a car like our friends' and putting the handmade wooden seat in the back
of the company pickup truck for my brother Nick and me—my sisters
Margie and Judy looking at their big brothers with wide wondering
eyes as we dressed up for our first teenage dates—my trying to convince
Nick it was *his* turn to milk Rosemary, the family cow—the countless
times I brought my school buddies home unannounced and saw Mama
happily set an extra place or two at the table—getting up early once in
awhile to have breakfast with Daddy before anybody else was up and
seeing his open Bible by his plate, as he eternally studied for his Sunday-
school class—and all the myriad little things: the moments of extra
affection, the ways that Arch and Margaret Boone demonstrated their
quiet love for their kids and their kids' friends—and for just about anybody who needed something they could give.

A real family, a real home, not fancy—but filled with love and lasting
values and personal concern, and a deep-rooted belief that God cared
about us. No matter how far back my memory carried me, He was al-

ways there, in that house, living with us and teaching us what life was really all about.

My heart filled with emotion, with love for this mysterious Father whom "having not seen, we love" (*see* 1 Peter 1:8), who had carefully brooded over us and met every need.

I began to talk to Him, to thank Him for His countless kindnesses, His abounding love poured out on us in the Boone family in that warm, old, frame house, to let my loving God know I could see something of the pattern He had woven through our lives, how painstakingly He had protected each of us, not allowing this simple praying bunch to be hurt too badly by our own mistakes. I loved Him so much in that moment, I wanted to tell Him so.

After a while, I ran out of words, and began to sing in the Spirit.

Still swaying gently back and forth in the warm evening breeze on the porch swing, I gave my voice to melodic praise of the God of all creation, allowing the Holy Spirit to direct the melody and to fashion the words as I poured out the flowing feeling of my heart toward my loving Father. I didn't recognize any of the words, and I'd never heard the melody before—but I knew they were the direct expression of what I was genuinely feeling, and the Spirit of God was helping me to say, "I love You, Lord" in a precious unfettered spontaneous way.

It was then I heard the crickets!

In what seemed an explosion of sound, as if someone had given a giant hidden chorus a distinct downbeat, hundreds of crickets were chirping and trilling—and all at once! I was surrounded, almost engulfed in the sound—and it startled me so, I stopped my singing and looked around.

I thought to myself, "What's going on?" I'd never heard crickets so loud in all my life. It was joyous and friendly, but so intense that I sat and listened for a moment.

And then it hit me: *They were doing exactly what I'd been doing!*

They were simply praising the Lord with all their might! Without the involvement of intellect, but obeying an instinct woven into all nature, those little creatures were "making melody in their hearts to the Lord" (*see* Ephesians 5:19) in a truly spontaneous, unself-conscious way. They had joined me in *my* praise, as if I'd given them the cue!

So I began to sing again, with the crickets.

I raised my hands to the Lord and really sang praise with my spirit, lifting a joyous anthem of unrestrained adoration to the God who spoke all things into existence and provides lovingly for all His Creation with limitless care—because He still looks at each of us with the same pride and concern He felt in the beginning when "God saw that it was good" (Genesis 1). *He still loves every part of His creation!*

The animals know it. The plants all know it. The stars and the planets testify to His great goodness, and the seas and the hills and the sun and the rain all vibrate with praise toward the Maker.

Only man, of all creation, is inhibited and stunted and mostly mute in his expression of love and gratitude toward the God who made him! Only man has turned away and largely denied the Source of his existence; and on the rare occasions when we "religious" people spend a few minutes in song or prayer or worship, it's often dry and self-conscious and programmed and manufactured, conveying precious little real love and devotion and emotional outreach of spirit to the Father of our souls, who genuinely delights in the praise of His handiwork.

I can't adequately describe what joy there was in that experience—for many minutes, the crickets and I sang together in a fantastic chorus of praise. I was utterly free in my devotion, just like my tiny friends, and I had the definite impression that the Holy Spirit was the conductor of our harmony, weaving and orchestrating a spontaneous symphony to the glory of God. *I felt like Adam!* It seemed a Garden-of-Eden experience, unstained by human pride and satanic ego twists, the most natural "right" kind of worship I've ever known, pure and real and innocent. I didn't want it to stop, ever!

But it did. Suddenly. In an instant.

I was still singing and worshiping, but I was surprised that the crickets had all ceased at once, again as if on cue. Why? For some reason, I looked at my watch . . . .

It was 8 o'clock.

Exactly.

I said, "Thank You, Lord"; and I went in to watch the Julie Andrews show!

Fantastic? Of course.

Unreal? No, it was very, very real—one of the most completely real experiences of my life.

Over and over, from Genesis to Revelation, God has demonstrated His affection for *everything* He created, and His desire for man to get in step again with the Eden plan, which provided for him to exercise complete dominion over every living thing (*see* Genesis 1:28), while yielding himself totally to the guidance and instruction of his loving Father.

In the beginning of human history, Adam walked naturally through all Creation, calling each thing by its name, rejoicing in each day's discovery and praising the Lord for His infinite variety and provision. I'm quite sure he communicated freely with the animals, and maybe even plant life. (Science has shown that plants flourish when words of love and admiration are spoken to them! Even today.) In Genesis 3, Eve has her famous dialogue with the serpent, and there's no hint that this was unusual; in fact, if situations like that hadn't been normal, I doubt that the Devil could have used this beautiful, subtle, and charming creature to influence Eve in her disobedience. If this kind of conversation didn't happen all the time, she would probably have run screaming to Adam! But she didn't; she carried on a languid, tempting afternoon's discussion with the beautiful animal about "that tree" in the middle of the Garden and why God might have selfishly wanted to keep her and Adam from enjoying its fruit.

Oh, I'll bet anything that they'd had many conversations before *this* one! In fact, the serpent's first statement (*see* 3:1–5) seems to spring right out of the middle of a dialogue:

Yea, hath God said—really, He *said*—really, He *said* that? You don't mean it—why, that doesn't make sense! You *know* He's not going to let you die—He didn't go to all the trouble of creating you just to rub you out when you eat a piece of *fruit!* Oh, come on now—I'll bet I know why He said that. The fruit is not only beautiful, and delicious, but I happen to know it will make you *wise*—like God *Himself*—and He's just afraid that if you eat it, and know everything just like He does, you may not need Him anymore. But that's silly; we both know that. Why, you'll *always* love God and want Him around; we *all* will. Go ahead, Eve. We've talked about this so many times before; you owe it to yourself! And you've got to help your husband get ahead, don't you? He's so slow and trusting and naïve, always talking to any animal that walks up, always stopping right in the middle of the night or day to sing songs to God (when *He's* probably not even *listening*) and carrying on like a child with crocodiles and crickets and cockatoos. Why, Eve, he's just got to grow *up!* He could be like God Himself, if he'd just quit being such a child and go on and eat that fruit—and so can you. Go ahead, Eve . . . .

Farfetched? I don't think so.

True, we have only a fragment of Eve's discussion with the serpent in the Bible, and we're used to hearing it in unfamiliar language—but the creature used by Satan in the downfall of man is described as subtle and cunning, so I'm sure he didn't jump out of the bushes like the bogeyman or a mustache-twirling villain in an old melodrama. Like all his other devices, Satan's technique right at the beginning had to seem so natural, so sensible, so appealing, so rational to the mind and emotions, that Eve just gradually ran out of objections, of resistance to her "friend's" advice.

Aren't we still like that?

Don't we still want to approach life in all its aspects—yes, and God Himself—on purely rational terms? Don't we believe the testimony of our eyes, ears, touch, smell, and feel, and our sensual emotions and thought processes almost totally? Has man really grown at all since he left the Garden?

No. In fact, he's shrunk. He's shriveled—and weakened—and paled—and sickened—till at last he's near to the final death God promised if Adam disobeyed. The serpent flatly contradicted God and said, "You shall *not* die!" And fallen, disobedient Adam may have believed the Devil for over 900 years. That's right; original man, created in God's image, was so incredibly strong and able and potent that *it took Satan 930 years to kill the first one!* Even after he gained the legal right to destroy human life, it took the Devil almost *a thousand years* to weaken and wear out and finally kill the original! And if you'll read chapter 5 of Genesis, you'll see that Adam was not unique; *all* the folks back

then were living seven and eight and nine hundred years! Read it—it's
a fascinating, incredible chapter in human history!

Gradually, of course, through the many centuries since Eden, Satan
has perfected his techniques, sharpened his claws, invented all kinds of
new virus strains of sin-sickness, and got life expectancy down to seventy
years or less. And I think in the years just ahead, that will drop sharply,
due to ecological and economical and population crises.

But man, incredibly, looks at his history and thinks he's *progressed!*

He points to airplanes and space travel and skyscrapers and libraries
and computers and all our technological wizardry, and laughs at Adam,
even denying his own "fairy-tale" origin. All this pompous scoffing, while
he finds himself riddled with cancer, gasping with heart defects, gulping
smoke into his lungs, trying to explain and cure the countless blights and
diseases that deform and cripple our children, and living in mortal dread
of being wiped out in a mindless act of nuclear or crazed human violence.

He discards or picks at the Bible, the Word of God, as if it were
some TV snack, some curious relic from the past, and eagerly devours
the humanistic philosophies of other dying blind men, entertaining himself into oblivion with *Clockwork Orange* and *Deep Throat*—and top-
less, bottomless, soulless depravity.

He seeks out and builds into a best seller every book or "mind trip"
that can explain away truth and God and Bible, anything that can make
plausible his own rebellion and sensual appetite and thirst for self-rule.
The psychiatrist confidently banishes guilt and faith as archaic concepts,
the educator makes a joke of Genesis, the scientist predicts man's eminent
ability to create life and control his own destiny—and many, many religious leaders try to find "rational" alternatives for childlike belief in
every word of the Old and New Testaments, fabricating elaborate doc-
trines and theories to enable the so-called thinking churchgoer to recon-
cile his tenuous faith with the "practicalities" of fabulous and sophisti-
cated twentieth century living.

The Devil howls! Squirming on his belly, fallen forever from his high
place in heaven through his own pride and disobedience (Isaiah 14),
doomed eventually to a lake that burns with fire in eternal darkness, he
chuckles with demonic glee as poor sick and dying man still tries to
become "like God, knowing good and evil" (Genesis 3:5). What a ter-

rible, ghastly joke his Satanic Majesty has been able to play on man. In addition to atheistic, agnostic philosophies and governments, he has concocted countless "religious" systems *too*—for those who have to cope with that inner stirring *somehow*—that permit a form of ritual and religiosity that is socially and intellectually acceptable—*but* which cleverly discourage any real contact with the supernatural and living and miraculous Creator-Father-God.

Like a spiritual inoculation, he creates a minor case of religion to make the individual *immune* to the real thing!

Oh, what a charlatan, what a thief, what a destroyer, what a magician and deceiver our enemy is! Jesus thunders:

Ye are of your father the devil, and the lusts of your father ye will do. *He was a murderer from the beginning,* and abode not in the truth, because there is no truth in him. When he speaketh a lie, he speaketh of his own: *for he is a liar, and the father of it.* And because I tell you the truth, ye believe me not.

John 8:44, 45 (italics mine)

Two thousand years ago, the second Adam (*see* Romans 5) walked this planet, demonstrating to shrunken, weakened, blinded, stunted man what life was meant to be like. He cast out demons, He reversed natural processes, He confounded every intellectual system (especially the religious ones), and strolled on the water, appeared through closed doors, spoke to the wind and the sea—and they obeyed Him!

In His first sermon, He pointed to the lilies of the field and the birds on the wing—surely the crickets, too!—and spoke of the way God loves and cares for every living thing. Then He made the astounding promise that if any of us will *"seek first the kingdom of God,* and *his* righteousness"* (*see* Matthew 6:33), that same God will treat us even more tenderly and completely!

Then why isn't it happening? Why doesn't man rush to get in on an offer like that? Why does he willfully choose any and every conceivable course *but* God's way?

Because he's sick. Every single descendant of Adam has been infected, body, soul, and mind, with a demonic virus. He *cannot* comprehend

God's way, or accept His righteousness, which demands belief in the impossible, the *impractical* and the *absolutely supernatural* (Genesis 15:1–6). And since man, in his fallen and dying condition, still wants to accept the Devil's lie and approach God, even "in church," on a rational and practical and doctrinal basis—*"knowing* good and evil, like God"—he continues to compound the illness and hide the Kingdom of God even from those who are seeking it!

Listen again to Jesus, the last Adam: "Except a man be born again, he cannot see the kingdom of God" (John 3:3). Though the precious eternal Kingdom of God bursts into life all around him, blooming and blossoming and singing everlasting praise, if puny man insists on approaching the Creator through his own intellect, he cannot even *see* what's happening!

He's still subject to the fatal illness that killed Adam.

Look at the prophet Balaam in chapter 22 of Numbers: though he was a "religious" man, and had truly heard the voice of God and spoken His Word in the past, he became so blinded by his own reasoning and motives that when a fantastic miracle of God began to explode around him, *he didn't even seem to notice it!* When the ass he'd been riding refused to go any further and began to *speak* to him—under the anointing of the Holy Spirit—Balaam was so enraged at the apparent rebellion of this dumb animal that he beat it mercilessly, and engaged in a foolish and heated discussion with it, becoming much like an ass *himself! (See* v. 30.)

And all this time, *he did not perceive the Kingdom miracle* issuing from the lips of the humble barnyard beast. Proudly, obstinately, operating on the level of his own understanding, he came within a foot of his own destruction—till a second miracle happened and *"the Lord opened the eyes of Balaam,* and he saw the angel of the Lord standing in the way, and his sword drawn in his hand: and he bowed down his head, and fell flat on his face" *(see* v. 31).

A supernatural spiritual awakening had to take place before Balaam could see the Kingdom of God! Otherwise he was doomed, though miracles were happening right in his path.

Jesus said, "Except a man be born again—spiritually wakened—he cannot see the kingdom of God."

Paul said, "The man without the Spirit does not accept the things that come from the Spirit of God, for *they are foolishness to him, and he cannot understand them,* because they are spiritually discerned" (*see* 1 Corinthians 2:14 NIV).

Adam conversed with animals and had dominion over every living thing; God spoke to Moses from a bush that burned but was not consumed; through Moses' *spiritual* submission, God changed rods to serpents and water to blood and parted the sea and gushed water from rocks and even stopped the course of the sun for nearly a whole day (Joshua 10:12–14) demonstrating over and over *the power of the supernatural over the natural;* the ravens came daily to bring food to Elijah (1 Kings 17); the giant fish became Jonah's prayer closet and a huge plant, or gourd, grew up overnight to shield him; David's Psalms are filled with his exhortations, by the Spirit, for the mountains and cedars and rivers and every creature that draws breath to actively praise the Lord—and Jesus teaches us to learn from the sparrow and the lily and the mustard seed and the fig tree.

But man's too "smart" for that.

And so, demanding to know "good and evil," to be like God in his own mind and accomplishments, he dies. Like Adam.

But, oh, friend, listen once more to the *second* Adam, Jesus:

Believe me when I say that I am in the Father and the Father is in me; or at least *believe on the evidence of the miracles* themselves. I tell you the truth, anyone who has faith in me will do *what I have been doing. He will do even greater things than these,* because I am going to the Father. And I will do whatever you ask in my name, so that the Son may bring glory to the Father. You may *ask me for anything* in my name, and I will do it. If you love me, you will do what I command.

See John 14:11–15 NIV

I'd love you to take about five minutes and just stare at those words —and think about them.

Go ahead. I'll wait.

Look especially at verse 12, "Anyone who has faith in me—will do what I have been doing" (NIV).

What *had* Jesus been doing?

Skim over the preceding chapters of John again, and you'll see the most fantastic display of miracles and supernatural happenings that have ever blitzed the mind of man on this planet, including the raising of Lazarus from the dead—after four days in the tomb! That's what Jesus had been doing.

And then try to digest the rest of the verse: "He will do *even greater things than these.*"

Who will do even greater things? *"Anyone* who has faith in me." (Italics are mine.)

Shall I wait some more?

Friend, I know it's heavy. It's unbelievable, incomprehensible, unfathomable, absolutely preposterous. I'm sure glad *I* didn't say it!

Jesus said it— and He had a funny habit of saying just exactly what He meant. I don't believe He was exaggerating in those last moments leading up to the supreme test of His *own* faith and submission, His death by crucifixion and willing surrender to the Prince of Darkness and the tortures of hell for *our* sins.

I guarantee you, He was weighing every word and speaking just as plainly as the Son of God could speak. I sense a profound urgency in His words—a pleading: "Now don't let Me down, My brothers—I've shown you what life can be like. Every day of My ministry I've demonstrated the way our Father wants *you* to live, the way Adam was created to live, what it means to be created in the image of God. And with My own sinless Blood, I'm opening the way back to Eden, to the Tree of Life. Come home, believe, and live My kind of life. I'll show you a *miracle a day, every day,* and lead you into even greater triumphs over Satan than you've seen so far—because I'm going to My Father, and won't be bound by this single human body. I'll live My life on—in *you,* in *your* bodies!"

He had said to Martha, just moments before He raised Lazarus from the dead (John 11), "I am the resurrection and the life: He who believes in me will live even though he dies; and whoever lives, and believes in me will never die . . ." (vs. 25, 26 NIV). And to prove those incredible words, He walked to the tomb—the final destination of the original Adam and every single soul who ever believed the Devil's lie and disobeyed God—and commanded in a loud voice, "Lazarus, come out!" (v. 43).

And in the dark recesses of that chilly grave, Satan's own clammy kingdom, a spark was ignited; a lifeless, already decomposing body stirred; brain cells that had deteriorated and run together reassembled by the millions and sounded BATTLE STATIONS! screaming commands to every part of that lump of clay already returning to the dust from which it came. There was an onrush of new blood through veins that had hardened and dried; muscles that had atrophied suddenly tensed with life and a heart that had shrunk into a flaccid knot began to thud and thump with an authority that sounded like hideous thunder in the pit of hell—for *Lazarus'* death-clogged ears weren't the only ones who heard the mighty command of God's Son. *The Devil and his legions* heard that shout, too, and they were paralyzed with the cataclysmic realization that *it had begun!* Jesus, the second Adam, was reversing the process that it had taken Satan thousands of years to perfect, moving with supernatural power and reestablishing *dominion* over "every living thing," over the whole natural creation—and in the flesh of puny human beings!

He had to stop it—but he couldn't! Lazarus obeyed the simple command of Jesus and walked out of the open tomb, and not all the demons in hell could prevent it!

And though all his fiendish hordes worked night and day after that to destroy this *Life-Giver* before He could spread this epidemic of miraculous dominion, Jesus said to a crowd in Jerusalem who had just heard the voice of God thundering from heaven:

Now is the time for judgment on this world; now *the prince of this world will be driven out.* But I, when I am lifted up from the earth, will draw all men to myself.

See John 12:31, 32 NIV

How? How would "the prince of this world," the deceiver who had wrested dominion over this world from the one for whom it had been

created (Adam) be driven out—as Adam himself had been driven out
of the Garden thousands of years before (Genesis 3:24)?

By the *second Adam,* who believed and obeyed God, and who therefore had the authority to reverse the "natural" process and *recreate
men in His own image* (*see* John 3:3)—and to give *them* daily supernatural, miracle-working power to bruise the serpent's head and utterly
vanquish him!

Take a fast, thrilling look at the way this whole human battle with
the Devil ends, and then we're through.

The great dragon was hurled down—that ancient serpent called
the devil or Satan, who leads the whole world astray. He was
hurled to the earth, and his angels with him.

Then I [John] heard a loud voice in heaven say:

> Now have come the salvation and the
> power and the kingdom of our God,
> and the authority of his Christ.
> For the accuser of our brothers,
> who accuses them before our God *day and night,*
> has been hurled down.
> *They overcame* him
> by the blood of the Lamb
> and *by the word of their testimony;*
> They did not love their lives so much
> as to shrink from death.
> Therefore rejoice, you heavens
> and you who inhabit them!
> But woe to the earth and the sea,
> because the devil has gone down to you!
> He is filled with fury,
> because *he knows that his time is short.*

Revelation 12:9–12 NIV

That's the way it all ends, my friend, this duel with the Devil. As
surely as if you were watching it live on the evening news, God shows
us the final outcome of this supernatural showdown we're in!

Satan is doomed—and he knows it. So do all his demons (*see* Matthew 8:29). They know better than you or I how this story will end, and just what fate awaits them—but you can bet your life that the Devil will fight with all his hellish fury to forestall his destruction, and *take you with him,* if he can!

He can read this part of Revelation, and probably has it seared into his consciousness like a cattle brand. He knows that God intends to fill this earth with men like Adam, created in His image and having dominion over every living thing, as at the beginning. He knows that as flesh and blood men and women regain their supernatural authority, won for them on the cross by the *second* Adam, he will be overcome and bound and banished forever to a lake that burns with fire. He *knows* that this is his fate, with all his demons and human hostages!

Is it any wonder that he's pulling out all the stops today, tearing society apart and wreaking violence on all humanity?

Can't you see why he's desperately attacking the family unit and the institutions of government and law, trying to bury the Bible and turn religions against each other, sometimes in bloody war?

Should it surprise us that he's spreading all kinds of mystic and occult religions, actually working religious signs and wonders through misguided devotees—and at the same time spawning an avalanche of pornographic filth and heaping millions upon the producers and artists and publishers of sadistic depravity in films, magazines, and records?

Do we really expect Satan to stand idly by, while growing multitudes of believers begin to read their Bibles and to act upon its every word? Can't you see him seethe with rage and fear as humble, ordinary human beings, clay creatures that we are, raise our hands and hearts to the God of miracles and begin to *experience the wonder-working power in the Blood of the Lamb?* Can't you hear the dark caverns of Hades reverberating with his blistering commands to step up the pace, to pervert, to divide, to twist and distort and dilute the teachings of Jesus and to convince men in every possible way that it won't work—that miracles are over—that Jesus' authority is lost—that reason and rational thought and modern philosophy and man's technology are our only hope?

What will happen to his demonic kingdom if thousands of Christians begin to operate in faith like *the seventy-two disciples* of Luke 10:17

who returned to Jesus in joy, proclaiming, "Lord, even the demons submit to us in your name!"?

Jesus said to them:

"I saw Satan fall like lightning from heaven. *I have given you authority* to trample on snakes and scorpions, and to *overcome all the power of the enemy;* nothing will harm you. However, do not rejoice that the spirits submit to you, but rejoice that your names are recorded in heaven."

See Luke 10:18–20 NIV

Satan knows that when this happens on a global scale—*he is finished!* Small wonder, then, that Peter warns:

Be self-controlled and alert. Your enemy the devil prowls around *like a roaring lion* looking for someone to devour. Resist him, standing firm in the faith, because you know that your brothers throughout the world are undergoing the same kind of sufferings.

See 1 Peter 5:8 and 9 NIV

Notice finally that John saw *two factors* combining to give believers victory over the Devil:

(1) the Blood of the Lamb
(2) and the word of their testimony.

What is "the word of their testimony"? Their doctrinal beliefs? No —the word of their testimony is the account of their individual triumph, on a daily basis, over the tests and traps and tricks of our mortal enemy, *in this life!*

Your testimony is your story; *your* chronicle of the way Jesus' Blood gave *you* victory over Satan in *your* confrontations with him! Your testimony is the story of how you learned the nature of the battle we're in, how you made Jesus' words part of your experience and His Blood your protection, how His Spirit in you enabled you to wage and *win* your personal battle with the Devil and his army.

Your testimony is the record of *your* miracle a day!

I've shared with you some of my testimony. But it's only a small part; the daily signs and wonders in the lives of my family are happening faster than I can record them. Oh, there are occasional setbacks and lots of obstacles—we know we're on the Devil's "get" list—but every day is a wonderful adventure, and each day brings us some fresh evidence of the loving power of God (*see* John 1:12), the assurance that our names are written in heaven—and that through Jesus Christ alone, the demons have been made subject to us as we use His authority!

It's not a conflict we take lightly. Though we don't *fear* Satan and his attacks—for "greater is he that is in you, than he that is in the world" (1 John 4:4)—we sure have a healthy respect for his awesome abilities and demonic genius. I'm not unduly afraid of rattlesnakes, either—but I take every sensible precaution to see that one doesn't have a clear shot at my leg!

Jesus' brother, Jude, in his little epistle just before the Book of Revelation, reminds us that even the Archangel Michael gave the king of hell a wide berth, calling on the Lord Himself as Defender.

How frightening to see non-Christians and mystics and spiritual opportunists advertise themselves as "exorcists." It's like little Pop Warner footballers jumping right into the middle of the Super Bowl! The seven sons of Sceva, a Jewish priest, found this out to their great sorrow; read about it in Acts 19.

In fact, read Genesis to Revelation—as often as you possibly can!

That incredible, precious, powerful, humanly unbelievable but eternally accurate Bible is the *Manufacturer's Handbook*—it's your defensive *and* offensive weapon in your daily skirmishes with Satan. It's the two-edged sword that Jesus took with Him into the wilderness to face the Devil (*see* Matthew 4), and woe to the person who tries to wander through life today without it as his guide and authority!

I pray that you are already recognizing your own *Miracle a Day*. They're happening in your life, whether you recognize them or not, and God is willing to do fantastic things for and through you, if you'll let Him. When you pray, *"Give me this day my daily bread,"* ask the Lord to give you manna from heaven, like He did for the Israelites—a daily portion of supernatural food, to build your spirit into His image.

He'll do it! He *longs* for human beings to test His word, to ask for more of His Spirit, to dare to grow daily in strength and grace and power. Oh, He longs for sons and daughters worthy of His Name!

Finally, *read Paul's "battle plan" in Ephesians 6:10–18;* it contains the winning strategy and our Quartermaster's provision for every single volunteer. It's completely up to the individual to enlist (there are no draftees in *His* army), and he'd better make sure he gets every piece of equipment he can!

And let your spirit soar on these words from our conquering, triumphant King, our glorious Champion:

> Peace I leave with you; my peace I give you. I do not give to you as the world gives. Do not let your hearts be troubled and do not be afraid.
>
> You heard me say, "I am going away and I am coming back to you." If you loved me, you would be glad that I am going to the Father, for the Father is greater than I. I have told you now before it happens, so that when it does happen you will believe. I will not speak with you much longer, for the prince of this world is coming. He has no effect on me, but the world must learn that I love the Father and that I do exactly what my Father has commanded me. Come now; let us go.

John 14:27–31 NIV